IN THE SHADOW OF THE SAN FRANCISCO PEAKS

Frontier Adventures
by Lou Bader

Edited by Joseph S. Karol

Published by
Light Technology Publishing
P.O. Box 1526
Sedona, AZ 86339

IN THE SHADOW OF THE SAN FRANCISCO PEAKS

Frontier Adventures

by Lou Bader

Published by
Light Technology Publishing
P.O. Box 1526
Sedona, AZ 86339

ISBN 0-929385-52-7

Library of Congress Catalog Card Number: 93-08768

Edited by Joseph S. Karol
Cover painting by Jessie Lang
Bronze on back cover by Lou Bader

Printed in the United States of America
Mission Possible Commercial Printing
P.O. Box 1495
Sedona, AZ 86339

10 9 8 7 6 5 4 3 2

DEDICATION

This book is dedicated to the brave homesteaders of Fort Valley. They seldom made the news but they did make history.

ACKNOWLEDGMENTS

My Wife, Emma Jean Bader
Philip Reed Rulon, Professor of History, NAU
Joseph S. Karol
Arizona Historical Society Pioneer Museum
Ruth Ann Border
Peter Bloomer
Silver Fox Studio

CONTENTS

Preface

Long before I knew Lou Bader was an artist of national renown, I suspected that the individual who fathered the community of Baderville had to be somebody who had an abiding interest in preserving the frontier heritage as well as a person who had a keen eye for natural beauty.

The architecture of the homes in the "subdivision" consists mostly of colorful, rustic replicas drawn from the Old West, with the predominant style the long rambling ranch houses that grow along with the family. Moreover, the geographic setting of the valley is as spectacular as can be found in the Northland. The Coconino National Forest is to the back, while the majestic San Francisco Peaks loom to the front. Green pines and wildflowers complete the landscape, making this section of the high country good for the soul and the body.

The author of *In the Shadow of the San Francisco Peaks* is as multifaceted as the region that produced him. He is a teacher, a sculptor, a radio and television performer, a director, a politician, a realtor and, in the pages that follow, Bader indicates that he is a historian as well. This book is a collection of essays that Lou wrote for the private consumption of friends who he thought would enjoy knowing something about the evolution of the community in which they lived. Many of the vignettes became conversation pieces in Flagstaff as well as Baderville, making it evident as early as 1985 that these reminiscences should be preserved for others, young and old, to read in the future.

The twin threads that knit the narrative of this book together are individuals and institutions: we read of boyhood chums, family, homesteaders, pioneers, mysterious strangers, and relatives, in addition to the teachers and priests and nuns who made the schools and churches an integral part of the daily social fabric. No tales of childhood would be complete without an array of animals, domestic and wild, and both are found here in abundance. But perhaps the most interesting and universal passages are those that evidence the impact of people on the land and of the land on the people. Our most famous historian in this country believed that the frontier was the force that colored and shaped the American character, instilling in us a sense of individualism, patriotism, and brotherhood. Thus, Lou Bader is in heady company as he provides yet one more case study of our pioneer heritage.

In conclusion, I hope that all who read this book will savor these stories and that the following words and pictures are ingredients that will stimulate a continuous appetite for the tales of Old Arizona.

Philip Reed Rulon

Introduction

Before I introduce you to the mountain boy and tell you how his stories came to be published, you should first meet his mountains. These are the San Francisco Peaks north of Flagstaff, Mt. Agassiz and Mt. Humphrey. The latter, at 12,670 feet, is the highest mountain in Arizona. It is visible under northern Arizona's azure skies for many miles around from all directions, to natives and to the millions of tourists who come from all over the world.

The Peaks are a shrine for Native Americans of northern Arizona, the Hualapai, Havasupai, Kaibab, Hopi, Navajo, and Western Apache. The last three tribes regard the Peaks as a dwelling place for the Katsinas, Yei and Gan, their tribal gods, and, they conduct sacred rites on the slopes.

Northern Arizona is and has been, for countless ages, Indian country. In the story about the school house, chapter eleven, the author recounts how he and the other pupils used recess time to look for arrowheads in the school yard. These could have been from a Cocohina settlement or camp near the headwaters of what is now called Rio de Flag, which forms the valley of Fort Valley. The Cocohina, after whom Coconino County is named, roamed this area as long ago as two thousand years. They were one of the hunter-gatherer bands who first drifted into the area fifteen thousand years ago, possibly descendants of those who crossed the Bering Straits thirty thousand or more years ago.

The Peaks are the edges of craters left from a 15,000 foot volcano that erupted eons ago. Reports that there is still some volcanic activity in the heart of the crater have led to stories about a monster that inhabits the place.

The name San Francisco was given to the Peaks by Franciscan missionaries who came to the Hopi villages in the sixteenth century. From their chapel atop the mesa to the northeast, the Spaniards could see the peaks and named them after their founder, St. Francis. By the way, the Hopi, who had no taste for Christianity, killed the missionaries, threw their bodies off the cliffs and drove out the soldiers.

New Age devotees regard the Peaks as an energy vortex, and a good number climbed the mountain on August 17, 1987, the day of the world-wide Harmonic Convergence. Thousands come here in winter to ski at the Snow Bowl, and many others come year around to hike and to camp and to explore the seven botanical zones that exist on Humphrey, from high desert to alpine.

Whatever the time of the year or the direction from which the viewer sees them, the Peaks are magnificent, an imposing and awe-inspiring sight. My first view of them was on a July day in 1974. I had endured the 115-degree heat of the Sonoran Desert in Pinal County, south of Phoenix, for several months, and was seeking relief, as do tens of thousands of desert dwellers every day in summer. Interstate 17 on Friday evenings presents a spectacle of an almost continuous line of cars from Phoenix to Flagstaff.

As the road wound higher and higher, I felt cooler.

Suddenly, at the 6,000-foot level, where the cedar and the yucca give way to the pine, I saw the Peaks. It was a clear day, with a deep blue sky arching over all the scene. There, ahead of me, loomed the blue-gray mountains, with a wainscotting of green tress three-fourths of the way up, a pale green in the full sunlight, set in the deep green of the surrounding million-and-a-half-acre Coconino National Forest. The scene resembled a turquoise brooch made of four colors of stone: light blue, dark blue, light green, dark green,

with the dark blue of the Peaks' tops as the central setting. Wispy silver clouds in back of the crater served as a frame.

I drove the car to the side of the road, stopped, got out and stood viewing the scene for I do not know how long. I made a vow that someday I would live where I could see the Peaks every day. I fulfilled that vow partially in the fall of 1985 when I returned from a teaching stint in Saudi Arabia and joined my wife, Kathleen, who had returned earlier from a similar job and was attending classes at Northern Arizona University in Flagstaff, working on her doctorate in school administration. I joined the English Department and taught composition.

We lived in the city near the campus, but the Peaks beckoned. I could answer their siren call only on weekends and holidays until December of '86, when we found a house to rent below the Peaks. The picture windows of that house framed a view of the Peaks. The rambling one-story frame structure was in a development called Baderville that adjoined the Coconino National Forest on the west. I found out that the house had been built by Lou Bader and occupied by his family and that he was now living down the road. The entire development was on what was once the family ranch.

Besides the location and the view and the good well water which came from a well that Lou Bader had witched, my wife and I found that another "perk" of living in Baderville was a free subscription to *The Baderville and Valley News*, an 8-1/2 by 11 inch newspaper of one sheet (sometimes two). This monthly publication had a grand total circulation of 130. It was written by Lou and edited by his wife, Emma Jean. Each issue carried Baderville news (nothing too world-shaking) and one or two stories from Lou's childhood or youth in Flagstaff or at the family ranch north of town.

Over the following months, as each issue arrived,

I became convinced that the stories deserved a wider circulation. As an English teacher, of course, I know a good story when I see it. The stories are charming and humorous, a reflection of the author.

One day I went to Lou's house and found him finishing up the chores with his horses and doves and ready to start in the greenhouse or the sculpture studio. I broached the subject of combining the stories into a book. Lou told me that he was writing the reminiscences for his grandchildren and had never thought of a wider audience. When I pointed out that no one else had written about the "good old days" in Flagstaff, and that he was the last of the old-timers, he agreed to do a book, if I helped with the editing. We shook hands on it and you have the results in your hands.

The mountain boy has come back to his childhood haunts and is now a mountain man. The stories are really Lou Bader's autobiography, just as the bronze grouping on the lawn of the Flagstaff City Hall, which depicts a mountain man protecting a fawn from an eagle, and which he sculpted and donated to the city, is his autobiography in bronze.

Joseph S. Karol
Instructor of English
Northern Arizona University
Flagstaff, Arizona
June, 1988

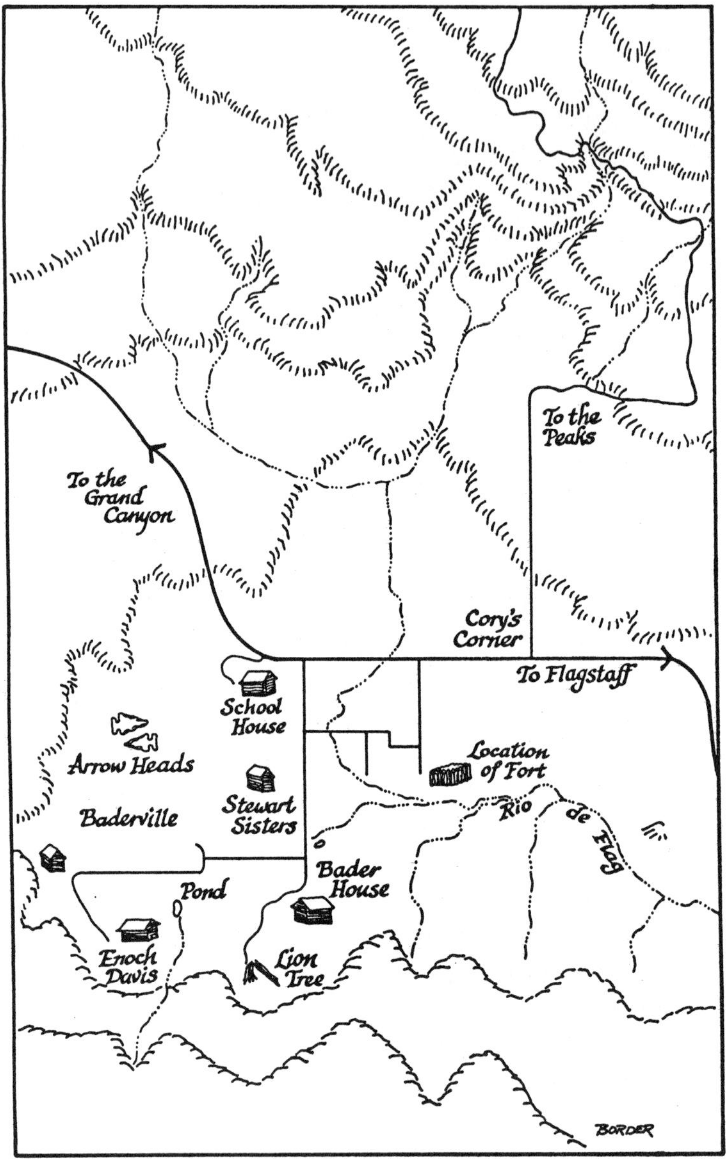

Baderville, Arizona

Fort Valley Road Still Holds Its Charm

Thousands of times I've traveled over Fort Valley Road, and still it has not lost its charm. We first started our many journeys to the valley area 70 years ago. We – all seven kids, and mother and father – would crowd into our tin Lizzie pick-up and start out for what was then known as the Bader Ranch.

The little grove of aspens on the first curve looked pretty much as it does now. The Rio de Flag, unencumbered then by check dams, would be a rushing torrent in the spring. Just before we would arrive at the big curve in the river, those in front would crawl up on the seat, and the kids in the pick-up bed would climb up on the wooden side rails to keep our feet dry. Father would nurse the old Lizzie across the stream. Then we would all jump out and help push the truck up the hill.

The beauty of this area and many pleasant memories were the chief motivating factors for my return to Flagstaff.

During the past 25 years, my child bride and I have traveled this route several times a day. We are still thrilled by its loveliness.

Lou and his father at the homestead cabin

Early Life in Fort Valley

I thought that the folks in Fort Valley would like to know something about early life in this area. My family acquired our ranch, as we called it, about 65 years ago. Although we had a house in town, we enjoyed coming out to our two-room cabin, and we spent much time there in the summers. In a spirit of fun we called it Baderville. I never dreamed that it would expand to the size it is now.

Life was pretty rustic. Our wells were hand-dug, and the water was obtained by dropping a bucket on a rope into the well. This took a little doing; you held the rope, and grasping the bucket on a slant, you let it go.

The weather was quite different then. Flower gardens and vegetables could be grown outside. We had carrots, turnips, peas, and potatoes. Chickens, too, added to our larder.

We had especially good luck growing potatoes in this virgin volcanic soil. The following is a news item my mother clipped from the *Coconino Sun* around 1918: "A.G. BADER SHIPS TEN CARS OF SPUDS."

The raising of potatoes is becoming a point of discussion throughout the county. Nowhere in the western states is a place to be found where spuds with the size and quality of the local variety are raised.

"In the past several days, A.G. Bader (my father) has shipped three cars per day from this locality. The ranchers of this vicinity are enthusiastic about the potato industry, and look forward to next year as being better than before.

"With the success so far attained, they believe the next crop will be higher quality and worth from ten to fifteen cents more on the market." (That must have meant ten to fifteen cents a bushel.)

All the vegetables were watered from the well, but the potatoes had to rely on the rain god. This was called dry farming.

The little creek that flows through our ranch and down the valley ran most of the summer. It is only since the introduction of so many stock ponds that it flows only after the snow melts. We could even swim in some of the pools. Although the water was cold enough to stop your heart, we didn't mind.

There were quite a few water-dogs, and even a few crawdads to catch. This creek is a tributary of the Rio de Flag. After a good snowy winter it can still become

Lou and siser Jayne, fresh from Cincinnati

a respectable little river.

All this area was fenced by hand-split rails. These were split and installed by the A-1 ranch hands. Some must now be close to one hundred years old, including those salvaged and now in use at my home on Antoinette Way.

Of course the winters were long and tough, and extremely difficult to survive. In spite of this, a few people tried to make a year-round living here. In the future, I would like to tell you about some of these brave and wonderful folks.

Early History of the Valley

For those of us who enjoy this beautiful valley, it is easy to imagine how wonderful it must have been for the Indians who occupied it in the summer months, long before the white man came. We knew of this because of the many arrowheads and obsidian chips we found here as children, mostly in the area now known as the Experimental Station. Especially after a summer rain, we walked around in the forest with our eyes glued to the ground, and every once in a while we'd find a perfect arrowhead.

The center of the valley probably was a small lake. Arizona Engineers' test holes reveal round river rocks, smoothed by many a year in a small stream running into the valley, the same one that now runs in the spring. An altimeter check shows that the southwest corner and the northwest corner are the same elevation, making a perfect lake bottom to hold the summer rains and the winter runoff. It takes several hundred years for such a valley to fill with soil.

With all the cottontails, jackrabbits, prairie dogs, deer and elk, this must have been a paradise for the Indians.

By 1876, the Civil War had been over for more than a decade and the army had returned to Arizona. The arrival of Mormon colonists heralded the first permanent settlement in northern Arizona.

A pioneer settler, John Young, a son of Brigham

Young, contracted to deliver 50,000 ties for the Atlantic and Pacific Railroad (later to become the Santa Fe). He built a camp for his tie-cutters here in our valley. It was located at the south end of what is now Lake Trail. The threat of raids at the hands of Apache and Navajo warriors caused Young to turn the camp into a fortress. He called it Fort Moroni. A log structure approximately seventy-five feet long acted as one side of the bastion; the other three sides consisted of railroad ties set on end in the ground. A tent city was established inside the stockade. The Indian raids never materialized, however, and the fortress walls were eventually torn down and used for firewood.

The Homestead Cabin

After circumstances forced Young's departure, the Arizona Cattle Company, known as the A-1 brand, moved in and became one of the largest in this area in its day. A-1 had 132,000 acres of land, purchased from the railroad for fifty cents an acre. They built several new buildings at Fort Moroni and renamed it Fort Rickerson. During its heyday the Arizona Cattle Company, or A-1, ran 16,000 head of cattle on some of the finest cattle country in Arizona.

The head of ranching operations was a man named B.B. Bullwinkle. He erected fences, built barns and bridges and even strung a telephone line from Fort Rickerson to Flagstaff.

In the early 1900's, the owners of the A-1 sold the ranches to the Babbitts. The gentlemen from Cincinnati not only doubled the size of their ranch in one stroke, but acquired some of the best range in Arizona in the deal. Many of the barns and bridges and remnants of the fort were still here when the Corys, the Davises and the Baders came into the valley in the later 'teens.

Homesteaders

One of the first homesteaders who tried to make it in the valley was Enoch Davis. He was a large man in his early forties, with aquiline features, long blond hair and a large walrus mustache. The mustache was stained a beautiful burnt sienna. When he refueled his tobacco chew, he would take a solid slab out of his shirt pocket, and, with a very large knife, slice off a piece and cram it into his mouth.

The blond hair was quite long most of the time. When he did get a haircut, his diminutive wife would perform the deed. It looked as if she put a bowl on his head as a guide. There was a great contrast of color around his neck afterwards. The part that had been protected from the sun by hair was extremely white.

Lou, Enoch and Dolph

He almost looked like a different man. Enoch was probably one of the strongest men around. He could take a three-wire bale of hay and toss it up onto a wagon with what appeared to be no effort.

Ma Davis, his wife, was raising a granddaughter. She was about my age – seven or eight – and always wore a little starched sunbonnet when playing outside.

It seemed as if Ma Davis was always washing clothes. In those days, it was not easy. She made soap at home out of lye, ashes and home-rendered lard. The water was heated on the wood stove and poured into a wash tub. In went a rippled wash board and the dirty clothes. They were scrubbed with the soap, back and forth by hand on the board, wrung out again and hung on a line. There was never a time when Mrs. Davis' line was empty.

There were a lot of predators around. Some of the worst were skunks. They would get into the chicken coop and raise havoc, killing more than they could eat. Enoch was laying for them, and one day he spotted one in the pen. He grabbed his gun and shot him, but not before the skunk shot *him*. Poor Ma Davis wore herself out trying to wash those clothes. The odor never did quite leave them.

Enoch was also a homespun philosopher and would come out with some down-to-earth sayings. One I never forgot. He and a cowboy were shoeing some horses that had been in the pasture for some months. They had just finished shoeing the first horse. I asked if I could ride him and try him out. They put a bridle on him, and I jumped on bareback. I was going to show everybody what a wonderful rider I was. I took him down the lane, turned him around and gave him a kick. I expected to ride past them like the wind. However, the horse had a different idea. When we arrived where the other horses were standing, he turned sharply to the left and I continued on, plowing through grass and rocks. When I got back on my feet, Enoch hurried down and looked me over to see if anything was broken. I hung my head in abject humiliation. He recognized my plight, and consoled my by saying, "Don't worry, Lou. Anyone who tells you he is a good rider and says he has never been thrown off, is a liar." I felt much better and have applied this thought to many other aspects of life.

We did not have a cow. We got our milk from Enoch, who had several. Once I had to ride over to Davis' ranch and get a couple of cans of milk. The cans were clean lard cans, one larger than the other. The small one was inside the big one. They both had their lids on tight. I was riding one of the worst cow-ponies ever. He was small and scrawny and mean. My dad had called him Dandy, a most inappropriate name. As he trotted along, the small can was rattling inside the large one. This startled Dandy, and he started to pitch, and off I went into the weeds and rocks. Then I remembered what Enoch had said to me and felt better. I never did learn to love that horse.

Most of the cabins were sided with shiplap purchased from the mill in town, but not Enoch's. He cut pines from the nearby hills. He stripped the bark to the brown underbark. Broadaxing began with a chalk line twanged with a squaring chalk cord. Enoch stood on the log with a long-handled filing ax and scored a vertical cut to the chalk line. Then he stood on the side of the log and hewed to the line. The logs were then

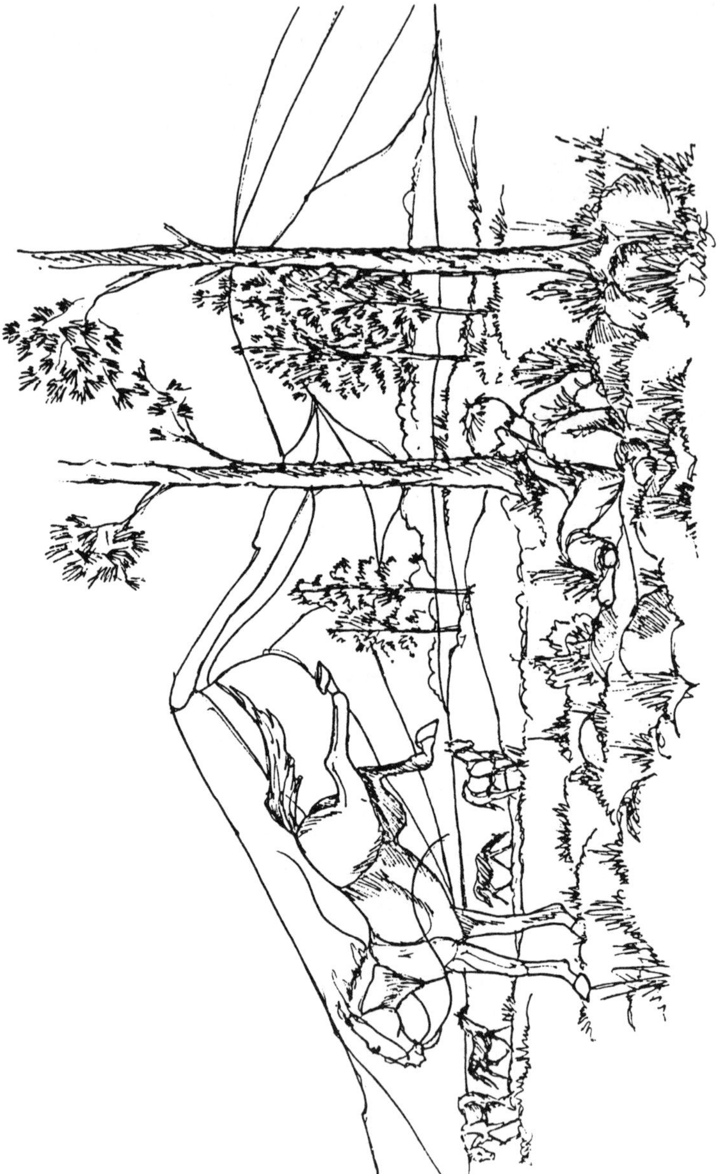

Lou and bucking Dandy

saddle-notched and gutter-adzed to round the notch. The logs were pulled in by the same horses that were used to plow the field. They were also used to help put the finished logs in place.

We all thought the cabin was a work of beauty. When it was finished, a celebration was held. There was fried chicken, stewed cottontails, homemade bread, apple pie made with dried apples and many other wonderful dishes. Ma Davis read a passage from the Bible. My mother said the customary Catholic grace, "Bless us, O Lord, and these gifts that we are about to receive."

After dinner, Jack Fuss, one of the most colorful persons in all of Arizona (and founder of the original Flagstaff Pow-Wow), played the guitar and sang. He had a lovely voice. He passed away recently at the age of ninety-two. We met him not long before that at the grocery store. He sang a little for us and he still sounded wonderful.

As the years passed, all the homesteaders moved away. Enoch's cabin started to deteriorate. In the summers, when we returned for short visits, we would walk over to see how things were holding up. Not long ago, when we went to look at the cabin, we found that it was gone. Someone had removed it. I wonder if they would have taken it if they had known the toil and effort that had gone into it, the hopes and dreams that Enoch had, and his desire to make a fruitful life for his family. I only hope it was not used for firewood, but instead has been restored somewhere and stands as brave and tall as it did in the beginning, and that Enoch Davis, wherever he is, can look down and know that a part of his heroic effort is still on earth. He was a real pioneer.

Making A Chalkline

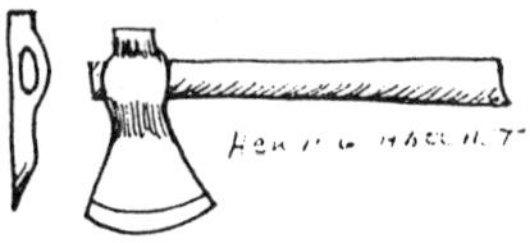

Hewing Hatchet

Scoring To The Line

Dogs

Hewing To The Line

Flat Side

Enoch's method of hewing the logs

The Stewart Sisters

Probably the bravest and most noble of the early people who moved into the valley were the two Stewart sisters. If ever there were proper maiden ladies, dainty and quaint, perfect prototypes of the spinsters depicted by a couple of actresses in the hit TV program "The Waltons," they were the ones.

The Stewart sisters were extremely well-educated and owned many books, ranging from Aristotle to Milton's *Paradise Lost* and would generously loan them to those interested with the admonition, "Please don't dog-ear the pages."

The sisters had given their nephew eighteen hundred dollars to construct a house. The nephew was a strapping, strong young man and an artist. The nephew's method of putting up a fence post was to sharpen the end of a log and drive it into the ground with a large sledgehammer. To my knowledge, he was the only person to use such a procedure. He was a regular Paul Bunyan.

He designed the house, and it truly was artistic, more like something the Walt Disney architects would construct. There actually were four levels: a dugout basement used for storing food, a living room and dining room, a kitchen, and two bedrooms, all on different levels. There was also a steep gabled roof and diamond glass in the gabled window ends. The door was specially made with a radius top containing a stained glass window. The window held the image of a peacock, a thing of wonder for me. I always half expected Hansel and Gretel to step out, or maybe I could walk up and get a piece of gingerbread from them.

The sisters were shocked that the cost of this house was the astronomical sum of eighteen hundred dollars. They couldn't imagine how their nephew could have spent so much money on the building, and they spoke about it every time they had an opportunity.

Serving tea was an elegant ceremony, with thin china cups and saucers and genuine silver spoons. The sisters were very frugal. When they had boiled eggs, the still-hot water was used to make the tea. Being spinsters, they would always remove the embryonic spot in the egg before eating it.

The small woodstove, which stood upright and was somewhat a family heirloom, had isinglass in the door. You could see the flames flickering and it was always a wonder to me that the stuff didn't burn. There was also a compartment for cooking bread and other things. Mostly they had a pot of chicken or beans on the top of the stove. Anyway, there was always a magnificent smell of something good. The Stewart sisters were always good for a handout of cookies, so I made a point of visiting them often.

The ladies were both tall and slender, and each wore her hair in a bun on top of her head, in a very regal manner. They were adorned with fancrest half-circle combs I had never seen before. Since I had never heard of costume jewelry, I thought the jewels were real, so I knew the sisters had to be rich, especially if they could afford a house that cost eighteen hundred dollars.

Mother and Dad on the road to the ranch

The rest of the family (Left to right: Adolph, Dorothy, Pearl, Edith and Katherine)

After the nephew finished the house, he took off and the hired man, Fuller, did all the manual labor. Small chores, such as collecting eggs from the hen house, were allotted to myself or the Cory boys.

Finally the sisters found it impossible to remain in their dream house and were forced to leave.

As the years went on, when we visited the ranch in the summer we could see the house's gradual deterioration. The beautiful door was gone, the diamond-shaped windows were missing, dust and dirt were drifting in, and the split rail fence that was on both sides of Bader Road was taken away rail by rail. We always made it a point to walk in and look around. I could imagine that the aroma of cookies or chicken soup still lingered and almost expected to see a pot of tea on the stove.

A few years back, by intention or by lightning stroke, the house burned to the ground. That was a sad day; it was such a great contrast to the other simple structures in the valley. To this day, as I ride past on the now-paved road, I glance over to see the Stewart sisters' house. In mind's eye, I do see it.

Fuller, the Hired Man

Fuller was not a homesteader, but he was a great help to all who lived in the valley at that time. He was known as "the hired man." He was, of course, many more things, an entrepreneur of many facets. His main occupation was hauling material in his wagon, pulled by his wonderful horses.

Most horses in those days were broom-tail mustangs, pinto, paint, or plain brown, descendants of the early Spanish horses, Andalusian and Bard. There was not a hot-blood among them; most of them were one step from being wild. It always amuses me to see painting and sculpture by cowboy artists, the frontier saddle and gear authentic down to the last buckle, but the cowboys riding Arabian horses.

Fuller's horses were outstanding because they were a matched team of draft horses, probably a mixture of Percheron and Clydesdale. This was very unusual in this part of Arizona, except for the horses used in logging.

Everything he did was of great interest to me. I was always hanging around, begging to be allowed to sit on the horses while he was going about his work. Their backs were so broad, that my short legs struck out at a 90-degree angle.

The wagon floor consisted of loose two-by-fours. The method of unloading dirt, cinders or other material was to remove the two-by-fours one at a time and have the stuff fall to the ground. When the horses stopped at an angle to the wagon, a large crack would appear in the wagon bed. When the horses started up and straightened out, the crack disappeared.

I climbed into the back of the wagon one day when the crack in the bed was open. Fuller turned around and said, "Don't put your leg in that crack." He turned away, and I promptly stuck my leg into the crack. He started up the horses, I let out a yell. He stopped the horses and backed them up, and I removed my leg. He did not scold me, but I am sure that about that time he was getting pretty tired of me.

Fuller was a black man and a staunch Baptist. One day we had stopped to water the horses at one of the stock tanks which were filled by runoff in the spring. Fuller looked over at me and asked, "Have you ever been baptized?" "Of course," I said. "You Catholic,

Fuller, Enoch, Dolph and Lou. Lou is not very happy about the cows being branded.

ain't you? When they baptize you they just sprinkle a little water on your head, ain't that right?"

"Yes."

"You need to be dunked in the water before you are really baptized."

I said, "I don't think so."

"If you die and they sprinkle a little dirt on your head, is you buried? Come here boy. I'm going to baptize you."

At that, I took off like a frightened rabbit.

Some time later, I saw Fuller, and he asked me, "Where you been, boy? I missed you."

I said, "I was afraid you were going to baptize me."

He laughed. "I was only fooling."

But that was pretty near the end of a beautiful friendship. I finally began to trust him again and enjoyed his company for many a year. I learned many practical things from him.

The Water Snake

It was early fall. The aspens had just started to turn yellow and gold, when John Jakle and I decided to make our scientific experiment. We were going to find out once and for all whether Fuller, the hired man, was pulling our leg. Fuller had told us that if you put a hair from a horse's tail in the water trough, it would turn into a snake. John had more of a skeptical turn of mind than I did. At that time of my boyhood, I had such an admiration for Fuller that I probably would have believed him if he had told me the moon was made of green cheese.

We had tried this experiment several times before, without meeting with any success. When we confronted Fuller with this fact he said, "You just haven't been going about it right."

He laid out the specifications for a successful snake creation. One had to get the hair directly from the horse's tail. It couldn't be just any old hair hanging around the stable. And the ornerier the horse, the better chance we had to accomplish the deed.

I certainly had a horse with the highest qualifications in that category, Old Dandy. Old Dandy had tossed me off his back so many times that I was getting very proficient at landing on my feet.

Dandy must have had a sad childhood, probably rejected by his mother or treated poorly by his siblings or other relatives. He had a suspicious nature. Just walking near him made him put his ears back. He acted as though he expected someone to hit him across the nose with a two-by-four any minute. All the efforts I had made to gain his confidence had failed. Dandy just didn't like anything or anybody.

Fuller also added that the hair pulling was best to be done after dark and the later the better. We wondered, would just after supper be all right? He reckoned yes. John had to add an amendment to that, since it was his custom to say the rosary each evening after supper with his Grandma and Grandpa. Fuller said O.K., but that was the last concession he would make and we were pretty close to blowing the whole thing again.

All during supper I was planning how I was going to pull the hair out of Dandy's tail. Coming up behind

Lou and Dandy at Enoch's Barn

him was about as safe as sticking your hand in a hornet's nest. After supper and the rosary with John's family we scampered over to the stable. I had thrown in a few petitions on the side, requesting that Dandy would be in a good frame of mind, but my first glimpse of him told me that my prayers had gone unanswered.

He looked over at me and back into the corner of the corral. I knew his thoughts: "Here comes that little kid I love to throw off my back." We chased him around the corral several times and finally managed to get a halter and rope on him.

I told John to lead him out from the corral fence so that I could approach from the rear and grab his tail. After several tries, I finally got close and gave a tug. Dandy reared up on his hind feet and tossed John onto a haystack, while I was thrown into the corral fence. Climbing to the top of the fence, I triumphantly held my hand in the air, displaying several horsehairs. We felt sure we had followed all the rules to the last letter. Nothing remained but to place the hair in the horse trough and await the result.

Every day after school we would hurry to the horse trough hoping to discover a snake. But day after day, no snake.

One day, when approaching the stable, we discovered Fuller delivering some hay. This was our chance to tell him what we thought of his horsetail story.

Fuller declared that we should not get discouraged. Had we checked today? Not expecting anything, we walked over to the horse trough and saw, to our amazement, a small water snake swimming around and trying to escape.

"We did it," we shouted.

Fuller came over and said, "I told you so."

We caught the little snake and as we walked over to the small pond to release him, John said, "Do you think old Fuller put that snake in the horse trough?"

I did not think so. I said, "Couldn't you see how happy he was when he walked away? Why, he was so pleased. In fact, he was laughing out loud."

Hunting and Fishing

I had been out before with my dad on many hunting trips. He was an accurate shot. There was much protocol connected with his hunting, a spin-off from his own father who spent many hours hunting in the Black Forest in Germany. There, one not only wore the proper clothing, but selected the right gun for the particular quarry. A rabbit could not be shot unless it was running, nor a bird unless on the wing – that is, when flying.

My father instructed me to aim in front of the rabbit so that he would jump right into the bullet.

When we went squirrel hunting, my job was to go on one side of the tree to frighten the little fellow and cause him to scamper to the other side. There my father would take dead aim, and sure enough, ka-plunk, down would come the squirrel.

All this technique was wasted on me, as I never took up hunting. It always bothered me to see anything shot, as I was deep into the stories by Burgess and never was quite sure that the rabbit for supper was not Peter Cottontail. However, I must admit that it never kept me from enjoying the repast.

On day my father announced that he and my older brother, Dolph, were going fishing and he figured that I was old enough to go along. What a thrill this was for me! I had heard about fishing and looked upon it as a great opportunity to prove I could add to the family larder.

The night before the fishing adventure there was a lot of talk about hooks and bait. Paraphernalia was spread all over the living room floor. Instructions were given about the proper approach to the fishing hole. No noise was permitted, as the fish were very skittish, especially if they became aware that someone was after their hides. I was shown how to bait a hook. I settled on using salmon eggs, as I could not get myself to stick a hook into a squirming worm.

Since we were camping out, clothing, blankets and a lot of vittles were checked in along with an iron pot called a Dutch oven. This was used to bake biscuits and, hopefully, fresh fish.

That night I could hardly get to sleep. I told my sister, Jayne, that I was sorry she could not go with me, but this trip was only for men. She said I was not quite big enough to be called a man, but I was too happy to quarrel about that.

After a good breakfast, early the next morning, we loaded up the back part of our Tin Lizzie Ford and were off to the stream. An eternity later we reached a spot for the night's camp that met with my father's approval.

Methodically, he proceeded to construct a camp. Cutting down pine branches, he made a lean-to which was covered with canvas. My brother and I gathered rocks to make a wonderful fire pit.

Dad whipped up batter for hot biscuits, put it in the Dutch oven and the whole thing into the hot coals. When the biscuits were done, bacon and eggs were added to the menu. Nothing ever tasted so good. I was even allowed to drink a cup of coffee. This made me believe I had really arrived at manhood. The coffee did not keep me from falling asleep as soon as my head hit the pillow. I felt very snug looking up at the stars, or watching the glowing coals, but like all little boys I had a harder and harder time keeping my eyes open. I hardly had time to say goodnight before I was a goner.

Next morning, after a hearty breakfast, we started our journey up the stream, loaded down with rods and reels and an optimistic wicker basket called a creel, to hold all the fish we were going to catch.

When we came to a little canyon branching off the main stream, my brother, who was very familiar with this terrain from earlier trips, suggested I explore this small stream. He knew full well I was in for a pleasant surprise.

Big Lou turned cowboy

While walking up the creek bank I fantasized about the very large fish I would catch. I envisioned my picture in *The Coconino Sun*, holding my large catch by the tail, with my hand inside my bib overalls striking a Napoleonic pose, and the caption "Louis Bader breaks all records for large fish."

Deep in thought I came around a bend of the stream to see one of the most startling and beautiful sights of my life. A gorgeous waterfall, very thin but wide, was flowing over a cliff with fern and wildflowers around the edge, cascading into a pool about fifty feet wide. It was so clear I could see the bottom where there were a lot of miniature fish scampering about.

For several minutes I just stood there and drank in the scene. Eventually realizing my quest was to catch fish, I took out my salmon eggs, put one on the hook and cast my line. After three or four tries something like an electric shock grabbed my arms, and I knew I had a fish.

Pulling in slowly and winding up my line at the same time, I drew out the most beautiful creature I could imagine. He had a rainbow along each silver side. The sun caused sparkles like small diamonds in the water drops on his scales. I stood and stared, finally comprehending that this was a live creature and that I had to make a split-second decision. Quickly, I released the hook from his mouth and gently lowered him into the water. He remained stationary for a while. Just when I thought I had done him in, he flicked his tail and disappeared, much to my relief.

That night we sat beside a warm campfire and feasted on fish my dad and brother had caught. I mused that I would never be a fisherman and, after all, who wants an old stuffed fish over the mantle? Besides, that huge fish I could have caught probably would have scared my five sisters half to death.

Purp nipping at the heels of the mountain lion

A Narrow Escape from a Mountain Lion

Around the turn of the century, mountain lions were numerous in the Flagstaff area. However, only once was I fortunate enough to get a close-up view of one of them. That episode is printed in my mind in indelible ink.

In those days the cattlemen and sheepmen thought that the only good lion was a dead lion. Whenever a calf or a sheep was killed, the deed was credited to or blamed on the cougars, and a bounty was placed on their heads. There were no professional hunters in the area, but whenever a cowboy saw a lion he took a shot at it. Nevertheless, the lions managed to survive very well until ranchers began to hunt them with trained hounds and some people took it up as a sport. Today they are pretty well wiped out.

My father once traded a sack of beans and a sack of flour, along with a slab of side-meat, for a magnificent lion skin. It had a beautiful head with its mouth wide open, displaying marvelous white teeth. The teeth had been implanted in flesh-colored wax. We little kids picked away at the wax gums until some of the teeth fell out. This made the lion look more ferocious than ever. The tanned skin was lined with green velour which extended beyond the edges and looked quite elegant. It was a spectacular sight to behold, spread out in front of a roaring fireplace.

The mounted skull made a perfect headrest for a youngster lying there basking in the glorious heat on a cold winter night. I had fantastic thoughts about how I would one day track down a lion and tame him.

Visibility in the clear pine-scented air of Baderville Ranch stretched out to the entire valley, ending only at the border of the trees. The whole valley was empty except for a feed barn and a couple of cabins. Our cabin was on the fringe of the forest. The view from our front door included the incomparable San Francisco Peaks. The back door opened into the wilderness. To me, it was only our back door, but from it country fanned out for many square miles. I knew there were lions around if I could just find them.

I spoke to my friend Fuller about this. He reckoned that it wasn't possible to really tame one of those wild critters. But if I wanted to see one, I would have to learn to track animals. This wouldn't be easy, but if I were willing he would give me some pointers.

I announced enthusiastically that I was ready to start learning to become a tracker.

He said, "The first thing you got to do is to practice keeping quiet, to keep your mouth shut, and not to jump and squirm around." He thought this would be especially hard for me. But if I could sit still long enough to get a bird to come and eat out of my hand, then I would be qualified to start to learn tracking.

I thought quickly. "Would a chipmunk do as well as a bird?"

Fuller thought it over and agreed. But it must be a tree chipmunk and not one of those critters that lives in the ground.

I was not about to tell Fuller that I had a chipmunk

pretty well tamed. I passed his test a few days later.

Out with Fuller in the woods soon after, I spied large footprints. Thinking it must be a wolf or the largest coyote I had ever seen, I drew Fuller's attention to it.

He said, "No, that's a big dog. You can see where he startled a rabbit and chased him to that big hole. You can see where he tried to dig it out. A coyote is too smart to waste his time that way."

As time went on I became more and more proficient. My biggest excitement was when I tracked a doe jackrabbit to her nest and disturbed her entire brood which scampered in all directions. Another time I tracked a badger to his den. I poked into the burrow with a stick and he let out a growl, which made me back off in a hurry.

I learned to notice where deer had browsed on the small trees and where the wild turkeys had roosted. By just sitting quietly by a water tank in the early morning I could see deer and elk coming in to drink. Usually they were led by an old doe. I knew they saw me, but they paid no attention. When they had all finished drinking, the doe would give a signal, and together they would turn and leave.

One day, while walking in the woods with my dog Purp, I came upon a sight that made my heart start pumping. There before me were two of the biggest paw prints I had ever seen. They looked as big as my baseball mitt. I knew it was a lion. Now was my chance to get near one.

I could tell by the depth of the imprint in the soft earth that he had jumped down from quite a height, obviously from a rock cliff nearby. The jump must have spanned twenty feet. I clutched my slingshot and checked the supply of rocks in my pocket so as not to be caught without defenses. With eyes glued to the ground I began to follow the clear tracks.

It was apparent that he was in no hurry. Here he had stopped to scratch the ground and had thrown quantities of earth up against a tree. There were great claw marks on the trunk, with newly oozing pitch running down the side. I was sure he was in the vicinity.

Purp had wandered off, as was his custom. If I walked a mile he would cover at least three by zig-zagging back and forth.

I tracked the paw prints for quite a way and suddenly they came to an end. By walking in a circle, and expanding it each time around, I came upon his tracks again. He had jumped straight up to a large rock outcropping and then taken off in another direction. When I checked the top of the rocks I could see where he had lain down for a while.

I thought, "Had he been watching me?" I considered giving up and returning home. The thought of being chewed up by a mountain lion was not very pleasant.

Just at that moment I heard Purp barking vociferously. Picturing the devastating possibility of a little dog being slapped in the face by a porcupine's tail, I hurried toward the frantic noise.

Suddenly, I came upon the lion's footprints again. I began to follow, slowly checking each one. Glancing up now and then I could see a large pine that had been broken by lightning. The break was about ten feet from the ground. The long top of the tree had fallen but was still attached to the stump. Watching the tracks, I was getting nearer and nearer to the high stump. When I was about fifteen feet away I looked up and there, staring down at me, was the biggest mountain lion anyone could imagine.

It was as if I were frozen to the ground. I just stood there, not knowing what to do, scared to death. He was crouched as if to spring. All of a sudden, out of the forest came my little dog, Purp. He was about one-sixth the size of the big cat, but he had a heart as brave as any lion's. Running up the tree trunk that slanted to the ground, he startled the big animal.

The great cat snarled and gave a tremendous leap right over my head. When I saw him coming I fell to the ground. The lion disappeared, with old Purp not far behind.

I just lay there for a while, afraid to move. Not until I felt a wet nose and a generous slurp on my face was I able to rise. I gave Purp a lot of hugs and said, "Let's go home."

That evening my Dad asked, "What did you do today?" I wanted to tell him about my close call with the lion. But, afraid I might be forbidden to walk alone in the woods, I could only reply, "Nothin' much. Me and Purp just went for a walk."

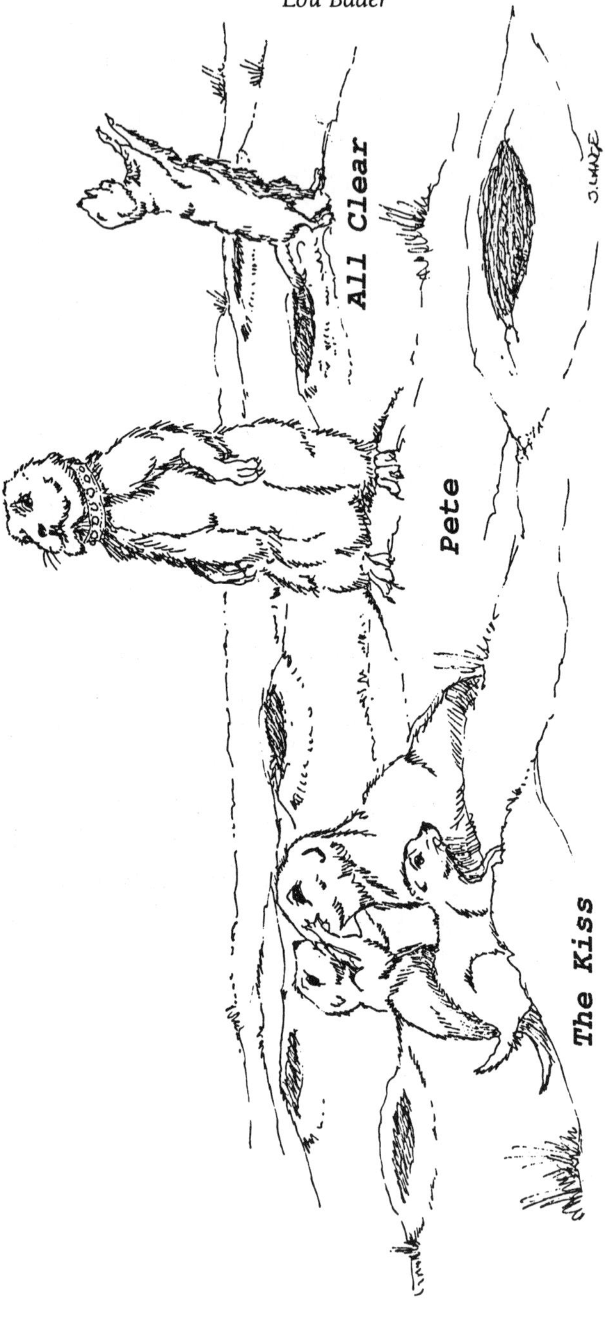

Prairie Dogs

Prairie Dogs

My father grubstaked quite a few Doney Park farmers. One day he asked if I would like to go along to bring some supplies to a farmer named Clark. Of course, I was pleased. First, we went to the livery stable and rented a small cart pulled by a single horse.

On the way out my father told me that Clark had said I could stay a couple of nights with him and his wife, if I would like to. He would come out the next following afternoon and pick me up. He said Clark was trapping prairie dogs, which were quite a menace to the local crops, so the farmers wanted to eradicate them completely. Perhaps I could learn something.

This disturbed me because I had grown very fond of these little animals. I had taught myself to imitate their "beep, beep" cry, and it gave me great delight when they would all look up and respond to my call.

Many an hour I sat quietly watching their antics, and the amusing little tricks they seemed to play on each other. They were very gregarious and had a strong community spirit. At all times during their day's feeding, a sentinel was on guard. At the least sign of an approaching coyote or hawk, the rapid danger signal, "beep, beep, beep," would go out, and immediately little brown figures would dart back and forth in all directions and leap into their holes.

Occasionally, I would give the sharp, quick danger

"beep, beep" just to watch them scramble and dive for their burrows.

Whenever the prairie dogs' paths crossed, they approached each other cautiously. If each recognized a relative, they appeared to kiss. If it were a stranger there was a bit of a scuffle and the interloper turned tail.

All summer they were busy gathering grass and storing it in their nests. I could not understand the great concern of the ranchers because I knew that such little fellows could hardly eat much.

I especially enjoyed watching the little pups when they emerged from the burrows. There were usually six, sometimes eight. The parents hovered over them like old hens. Whenever a young one strayed too far from the den, a parent hurriedly chased him back.

Once when a coyote held at bay a rather large male, I witnessed a display of great courage. Standing up on his hind feet, looking as menacing as he could, the dog feigned an attack on the coyote. He dropped down and rushed at the coyote, who fortunately was young and probably on his first solo hunting forage. The coyote retreated a few feet, and the prairie dog took advantage of this interlude to get a little closer to his burrow. Although I knew the coyote was just after his lunch, I was still pulling for the dog and was greatly relieved when he finally dove into his burrow.

That night at the Clark farm, while resting on a straw-filled mattress, I wondered what kind of traps were used. I soon found out they were steel—and cruel.

In the morning I followed Mr. Clark to where the traps were set. He carried a short club that looked like a pick handle sawed off to about twenty inches.

When we reached a prairie dog hole, I could see a stake driven into the ground, with a chain stretching into the burrow. Reaching down, Clark grabbed the chain and pulled out the trap. A large adult prairie dog was struggling to free himself. Clark raised his club and with one blow crushed the skull.

This was a devastating sight for a little boy to witness. I had never expected anything like it. I was shocked.

We checked the other traps and, since there were no more animals caught, we started back to the cabin.

While walking back, I planned that I would rise early the next morning, go to the traps, and free any animals that had been caught. I stayed awake half the night for fear I wouldn't get up before Clark went to check the traps. Just before the sun peeked over the horizon, I was dressed and running out towards the prairie dog village.

The first three holes that I checked had nothing in them. I considered hiding the traps. I didn't think that was proper and I knew my father would not approve. I was content just to spring them. Approaching the next hole I could see the tell-tale evidence of a taut chain. There must be a dog at the other end. I gently pulled it out to disclose an infant prairie dog pup. He was so small that when the trap tripped on his leg it was luckily caught in a space between the teeth. I released him. He remained quiet in my hands and did not try to get away. A hasty examination of his leg showed that he was not injured.

My first impulse was to let him go. On second thought, I told myself, "No, he might be trapped again."

I would hide him and take him home that afternoon when my father arrived.

In those days little boys wore blouses with a drawstring around the waist. When it was pulled tight there was a great space to hide cookies and other things. Quickly I opened my blouse and shoved the little fellow inside. Just then, I heard a gruff voice ask, "What have you got there, boy?"

"Nothing. I haven't got anything." I turned around to see Clark standing with his big club in his hand.

Just then the pup started to struggle inside my blouse. It was obvious that something alive was in there.

Clark yelled, "Do you have a prairie dog in there? Come here. Give him to me!"

He started toward me. I turned and ran. In a few strides he caught up with me and held me by my arm. I pleaded with him, giving all my best arguments why I should be allowed to keep the pup. He was little. I would take him away from Doney Park. Clark would never see him again. I was sure my dad would let me keep him. Talking as fast as I could, I finally persuaded the farmer to release me and let me keep the pup.

He said, "You can put him in that old rabbit hutch until your pa gets here. I don't want him running loose. One day you have one prairie dog, the next day you have ten."

As time went on Pete the prairie dog became quite an attraction in our neighborhood. He was permitted to run in the backyard of our house in town under careful supervision. He spent most of his time in a rabbit hutch, eating rolled oats and alfalfa. He became very tame, and would respond to his name.

I had managed to acquire a small blue collar encrusted with tiny fake diamonds and I put it on Pete. He accepted this and appeared to wear it with pride.

My father thought it was not right to keep a wild animal in captivity. He said that we should consider releasing Pete. After many discussions, I came to the conclusion that Dad was right.

Finally, the day came to release Pete. I was not about to give him his freedom in Doney Park, not with the memory of the traps still fresh in my mind. Dad was a little apprehensive about setting him loose at the Baderville ranch. He thought perhaps the prairie dogs there would not accept him. But I would not have it any other way.

We walked out into the pasture. I lowered him gently to the ground. With his little blue collar studded with fake diamonds glittering in the sun, he made an unusual sight to behold, to say the least. He appeared to be confused, but all of a sudden his instincts took over and he dove for the nearest prairie dog hole, only to reappear immediately with an angry old dog scolding him.

This was his first lesson in the wild – not to encroach on some other animal's territory. He scampered over to another hole and did not reappear.

For days afterward I looked for him, but in vain. Weeks later, I thought I would give one more try, and sure enough, there he was sitting on a large mound, still wearing his fancy collar, looking like a little king.

I called to him, "Pete, Pete." He looked up and came in my direction for a few feet, stopped, hesitated, came forward a little farther, turned and raced back to the mound. Looking closely, I could see why. Sitting next to him was a pretty little female. I said, "Why, you rascal!"

That evening my father asked, "Did you find Pete?"

"I sure did, and he has a beautiful little girlfriend."

My father laughed and said, "I would like to see the face of some old cowpoke when he comes upon a prairie dog wearing a blue collar studded with diamonds. By golly, I'm sure it will cause him to change his brand of whiskey."

An Old Country Schoolhouse

The little one-room school house at the Experimental Station in Baderville still exists. As you go into the property, keep turning, and there it is. I had the wonderful experience of attending that school in 1920. All grades were, of course, seated together. Our teacher was very kind and took a lot of time with each student. There were twelve students in all. I was in second grade and my sister, Jayne, was in third. It sure was great to have my sister to help me with the homework.

Some of the eighth grade boys were pretty big lads, at least so they appeared to me. At recess, there was not much to do. The boys mostly threw pine cones at each other or played marbles. No one was allowed to play for keeps.

The girls played hopscotch, a game in which they scratched some lines on the ground, making squares. They took turns throwing a piece of glass into the squares and hopped on one foot to pick it up and return to the starting point without falling over or touching a line. I wonder what happened to hopscotch.

Old Country Schoolhouse

The Livery Stable

In the years around 1915 to 1918, Flagstaff was a very small town, with a population of eighteen hundred, more or less. There were very few automobiles. Most people depended on horses and wagons.

Those who lived out of town usually rode their horses to work and left them at the livery stable during the day. The horses were fed and watered and had their feet trimmed or new shoes applied when necessary. It was the equivalent of today's service garage. Here you could also rent a horse and buggy for a day's outing in the country.

The main interest of boys in those days was horses. We always wanted them bigger and faster, and a cowboy was our special hero. I wore my brother's chaps and boots every chance I got, even though they were three times too large for me.

One day John Jakle and I, both about five and a half years old, were hanging around the livery stable. A big, mangy cowboy came in. He certainly did not look like Gary Cooper. When he smiled, his brown teeth showed and the two front ones were missing. His hair was matted, and the cowboy hat pushed way back on his head was stained with many years of sweat and dust. Most of the cowboys came to town in the spring for a yearly bath and to get dewormed.

To have something to say to him, I got up my courage, walked up in my most grown-up manner, and asked, "How do you break a horse?"

He looked down at me and said, "You climb up in the saddle, kick him in the flanks with your spurs, and say, 'Come one, you s__ of a b____, get going.'"

Well, this was the first time we had ever heard this expletive and we thought it was wonderful, especially if cowboys used it. So all the way back to the Jakle house we threw rocks and exclaimed, "I'm going to hit that s-o-b tree over there," or "that s-o-b stump."

We arrived at his home, and Maude Jakle gave us each a piece of buttered home-made bread. We were about to go back out and play when she said, "John, don't go out without your hat."

John turned around, and in his toughest cowboy manner said, "I don't want to wear that son-of-a bitch."

There was a moment of silence. It was then we both learned that expletives should be deleted. She asked me if I ever said that. I 'fessed up. She gave us each a good swat on the seat of the pants and scooted us out of the house.

John and I talked it over, and decided it was best not to use that expression around grown-ups, unless, of course, they were cowboys.

The Livery Stable

Paint

My brother, Dolph, was a superb equestrian. He rode bareback as if he were part of the horse. He had great admiration, love, and respect for these animals, and absolutely no fear of them. It was apparent when he was in the saddle that the horse was aware that Dolph was the boss. Occasionally, of course, he had to prove it the hard way when some old ornery broom-tailed bronco tried his best to dislodge him.

Contrary to the custom of the time, Dolph never used spurs or a quirt to force an animal into submission. Rather, he spent much time getting a colt used to a bridle. Then came a saddle, cinched up loosely and gradually tightened. Finally, he would sit in the saddle. When the colt was no longer in fear of these things, they went for that first ride. Mostly it worked. But whenever a colt had a different idea and started to pitch, he soon learned that the person on his back was there to stay.

Sometimes horse traders came in with their herds. They would set up a rope corral right downtown under the trees and put out the word that they were in business. A good number of the citizens always turned out to inspect the animals and start trading.

At one of these sales, my brother spotted a beautiful red and white pinto mare and fell in love with her immediately. The horse trader, sensing that this young man was completely under the spell of this exquisite bit of horseflesh, was quick to take advantage. He quoted what my brother thought was an astronomical price – two hundred dollars. The going price was fifty. Dolph, afraid that someone else would beat him to the purchase, left a deposit and hastened to borrow the balance from my father.

Brother, Dolph, on Paint - the greatest horse ever

When Dad heard the price, he was astonished. No horse was worth that much. He had to go take a look. Leaving Dolph in charge of the grocery store, Dad hurried down to the corral.

My father returned, leading a rather nice sorrel, and explained that this was a much better buy. Then, the only time in all my life, I saw revolt in my brother's eyes. No way. He had to have the pinto. Dad made a futile attempt to show him the more practical way, gave in, handed him the cash, and Dolph went flying back to the corral.

Not showing much imagination, my brother named the mare Paint. Now came the surprise. She had never been broken. The first time he sat on her she fell over backwards on him. It was only because of his prowess as a rider that he wasn't killed. Incidents like this kept happening, so Dolph decided he had to go about things another way and gain her confidence and good will with kindness.

Paint was not allowed to run in the pasture. Instead, she was staked out with a long rope which allowed her liberty to graze. Occasionally, we would change the location of the stake to give her access to greener pastures.

One day, walking home from first grade, I thought that Paint needed to be moved to a new spot of grass. I untied the rope, led her over to a large boulder, and thought, "Why not ride her?" Crawling up on the rock and maneuvering Paint near, I jumped on her back. Giving her a little nudge with my heels, I headed for the house. Without any resistance, she obeyed the pressure of the rope I had rolled up, allowing me to guide her into the back yard. When my mother responded to my call, "Come and see me on Paint," she turned white. No one had ridden that horse successfully before. Jumping off, I told her, "Well, I guess everyone can ride Paint now. You see, she is broken."

From that day on, there was a great change in Paint's attitude. She decided that things were not so bad. She would learn to behave and to fit into society, something that a lot of humans never learn.

Under my brother's expert hand, she was soon responding to every signal he sent her, no matter how slight. She appeared to take great delight in her new skills, and she displayed real intelligence when herding cattle. Once she knew where the cows were supposed to be located, she took over. No stubborn old "sooky" was allowed to have her own way. Paint was the boss and she let those cows know it. With it all, she was quick and nimble as a kitten.

My greatest pleasure was to be near her, to sit on her back. I would whisper in her ear and tell her that she was really my horse. I rode her every chance I could.

One afternoon I was assigned to keep the cattle in the lower pasture while my brother and some ranch hands were fencing off forty acres to plant wheat. I was allowed to ride Paint. They felt confident that she would not allow the cows to get out of hand.

The juniper fence posts had been installed and the barbed wire strung tight by tying it to the bumper of the tin Lizzie. That wire was so tight someone could play a tune on it. The men had finished their task and were headed for the barn when all of a sudden two big dogs came onto the scene and spooked the cows.

Those half-wild creatures started a stampede and headed for the newly strung wire, with Paint and myself directly in their path. The little mare made a valiant effort to change the direction of their charge, but soon we were engulfed by half-crazy beasts. Some of them were trying to hook Paint but, like a ballet dancer, she side-stepped and avoided their horns. The thundering herd passed us by.

When the foremost cows hit the fence, the wires broke like strings on a harp. The first few stumbled and a whole pile of beef fell on top of them.

Fortunately, none of them was badly hurt. By the time Dolph and the other men reached us, Paint and I had the cows going in a circle and we were starting to calm down.

Lou on Paint

My love for the pretty mare grew and grew. Each evening, I watched with keen anticipation for the dust that indicated that my brother and the hired hands were coming in. As soon as they arrived I would beg and plead for a few moments of riding on Paint.

To me it was like riding on a cloud, indeed, like riding Pegasus. I tipped the scales at under sixty pounds soaking wet, so I was nothing for Paint to carry. She could accelerate to a gallop from a standing start as if she were shot out of a cannon.

Long before the famous Indian Pow-Wow began, the ranchers held celebrations on the Fourth of July. Horse races were part of the fun, though they were not like the races we hold today. There were no professional jockeys and no allowances for the weight differences of the men were considered. It was each man and his horse, real life the way it was. The thought that a given horse had to be handicapped some way to even things up was ridiculous.

One evening at supper my brother announced that he was not going to ride in the races this summer. How would I like to ride Paint in the kid races? I couldn't believe my ears. I was sure I had died and gone to heaven. There was some protest from my mother, but Dad said, "Let him do it. He hasn't killed himself yet." My mother observed that it was only her prayers that had kept me in the world.

Now I had an excuse to ride Paint; we had to practice racing. By the time the event came about I was sure my brother regretted his offer.

Finally, the big day arrived. I was at the track a couple of hours ahead of time, brushing Paint, talking to her, adjusting her bridle and saddle over and over.

It seemed like an eternity until the kid races were fit into the schedule of events.

There was a race in which the riders headed for a certain destination, dismounted, took the saddle off, threw on another saddle, swished up, and took off for the starting point. The crowd yelled in great merriment at the antics of cowboys trying to milk a wild cow, using a Coke bottle as a container.

At last we were told to line up with our horses and the rules of the race were announced. There were six horses and kids. I had been sizing them up all morning and felt Paint and I could take them easy.

The man in charge came over and asked, "How old are you?" I replied, "Seven years."

He said, "I'm sorry, kid, you have to be eight before you can get into this race."

I said, "I'm seven and a half, and pretty big for my age." I threw out my chest and stood on my tiptoes.

I could see my brother putting up a good argument on my behalf. He shook his head, came over and said, "Too bad, Lou. We will have to wait till next year."

Up to this point in my young life, this was the saddest thing I had ever experienced. The remarks made by some of the other competitors didn't help. Like, "Don't worry Lou, your horse looks better in front of a plow, anyway." It was all good natured, but I was in no mood for kidding.

We remained until all the activities were finished. My brother hopped into the tin Lizzie and started home. I followed, walking Paint slowly, contemplating the evil turn of fate. While I was thus deep in thought, four of the boys that had been in the race came up behind me on their horses. They spoke good-naturedly and said how sorry they were that I had not been allowed to race.

All of a sudden I had an idea, "You see that bend in the road?" It was about a half mile away. "I'll race all of you there."

One boy said, "You're on," and gave his horse a kick. All four took off in a great head start.

I said, "This is it, Paint. Let's show them what we can do."

Like a bullet, she took off. I gave her a kick. She appeared to be flying. It was the first time I let her have her head like this and was she ever enjoying it. Soon we overtook all four horses and left them behind. As we went by I couldn't resist standing up in the stirrups to yell, "Eat my dust!"

As time went by, Dolph's other activities took more of his attention and I felt that Paint was more and more my horse. In fact, she was and we both knew it.

Early Flagstaff School Days

There were two grammar schools; one public, Emerson School (where the new library is now located) and the Catholic school, St. Anthony's, part of the old Nativity Church building. All of that is now replaced by St. Mary's. There wasn't much rivalry between the schools, although occasionally some of the public school boys would disdainfully call us "cat-lickers." We would yell back, "pup-lickers." I always thought they had the best of this verbal battle, because a cat-licker sounded much worse than a pup-licker.

The Sisters of Loretto were in charge of the Catholic school. They wore generous black gowns that covered the entire body, down past their high-top black shoes. They also wore an enormous white collar; it looked like a big bib. Head and throat were swathed in white. Straight down the side of each shoulder and across the head was a stiffly starched headdress that dipped in, becoming a heart shape over the brow. Over this, a filmy black veil fastened at the front edge with several black-headed pins.

This arrangement exposed not a wisp of hair. There was a wild rumor that the sisters had to shave their heads. I speculated on how peculiar Sister would look without her habit.

The voluminous pockets of the habit seemed to descend down to China. They were very handy places for Sister Alphonsus to keep confiscated marbles taken from big boys caught playing for keeps. This was considered gambling and was strictly forbidden. She would slyly slip these marbles to the little boys, taking care not to be seen doing so. Whenever she handed them to me, I was reluctant for fear of being seen and labeled Sister's pet. She continued to do so, and I carefully never mentioned this to anyone. This was my darkest secret.

The business of playing marbles for keeps was a cat-and-mouse game. It delighted the big boys to no end whenever they got away with it. Of course, no one ever snitched. That would have been contrary to the

On the way home from St. Anthony's school on Dusty, Father Vabor's house in the background

unwritten code of honor.

The boys and girls had separate play yards on opposite sides of the building. The girls were always released from school fifteen minutes early to prevent fraternizing with the boys. Otherwise, the boys might get nefarious or wicked ideas in their heads, like carrying the girls' books.

The school day opened with the singing of "Columbia, the Gem of the Ocean." I always thought it was "Columbus, the Jam of the Ocean" and sang it so, loudly. I was terribly disappointed when an unkind girl pointed out to me that it was "gem." I was sure "jam" was much better than "gem," and continued to sing defiantly "Columbus, the Jam of the Ocean."

Before classes we also said the Our Father and the Hail Mary. The Hail Mary's words included "blessed is the fruit of thy womb." I was curious what a womb was, so one day after morning prayer, I approached Sister's desk and asked, "What's a womb?" She turned red and yelled at me, "Go to your seat." While walking back to my seat I reflected that there sure were a lot of words you shouldn't say around grown-ups.

That afternoon, while walking home with my pal John Jakle, I asked him what a womb was. He replied he didn't rightly know, but he thought it was some kind of fruit tree that grows in Israel. Since John was the smartest kid in the class, I let it go at that.

Whenever I pass a present-day school I am pleased to see all the wonderful playground equipment. It was not like that in the early days. The kid who brought a ball and bat was always qualified to be captain of the baseball team. Those lucky enough to own a mitt were chosen to play ball. I was always the last one to be picked because I was not very good at it. I remember the captain saying, "I'll take Lou if you take two of those little kids." I was grateful that I was at least as good as two much younger boys.

The boys' side was covered with coarse gravel, which meant that our long stockings always had holes in the knees and our knees had ground-in gravel and large scabs that were constantly being broken open from innumerable falls. My mother would darn the holes and before the school year was over there was darning upon darning. The whole knee was one solid darn. Toes and heels developed holes, too. To mend those, she slipped a darning egg inside to sew across. It was a smooth egg-shaped piece of wood with a handle on one end.

Though the school did furnish two handball courts, each boy had to bring his own handball. At recess there was a real scramble to commandeer the courts. The fastest kid would reach the area first and yell, "First winners." He could then choose his opponent and the winner of that game would play with the next kid in line. John Jakle was not only a good scholar, but also a fine athlete and quite a sprinter. We worked out a system to outsmart our rivals. Just before the bell rang, John would walk up to the front of the room, supposedly to put something into the waste paper basket. At the bell he shot for the door. I would stand in front of the doorway and manage to hold back some of the boys just by being in the way. John would streak off to the handball court and pick me as the other first player. This worked fine for a while, until one of the big boys caught on.

One of these fellows was Neil Kuen. Neil had red

hair and there never was another face quite like his. It was covered with a multitude of freckles. You couldn't have touched his face with a match head without touching a freckle. In those days, if you didn't get a passing grade, you would be held back. Neil was twice the size of the rest of the boys and probably had been held back a couple of times. He took advantage of his superior strength to throw his weight around and bully the smaller boys.

One day after John had reached the ball court a couple of steps ahead of Neil, Neil gave him a shove saying, "Get out of here, kid. I was here first." A few back and forth shoves, and John realized the futility of continuing the struggle. He picked up a handful of

Jayne and Louis

gravel, threw it at Neil and, expecting the worst, turned and ran, with Neil in hot pursuit. I followed along, trying to think how to save John from total destruction because Neil had a cute little way of holding his victim by the neck while running his knuckles back and forth, with great vigor, in the hapless kid's hair.

Just as Neil was about to apprehend John, John fell to his knees and crouched down. The unsuspecting Neil went flying head over heels and plowed through the gravel, while John scampered for the safety of the schoolroom.

Not wishing to miss out on the magnificent humiliation of the school bully, I ran up to Neil and declared, "Do you know what your face looks like? You look like the cow ate some bran and pooped all over your face." This effectively added insult to injury and he came at me with murder in his eye. As he grabbed at me, I turned and ran for dear life. Since John's ruse of dropping on his knees had worked, I thought I would try the same trick. Falling clumsily to my knees and looking over my shoulder, I could see Neil rushing toward me like a freight train. Not to be fooled by the same strategy twice in one day, Neil aimed a kick at me. I moved quickly away and he missed and went flying into the gravel. This sight was so funny to me I started to laugh helplessly, and Neil caught me. He was about to deliver the coup de grâce when the school bell rang and I was saved.

I Learn About the Power of Prayer

I cannot remember when I could not read. My mother was responsible for this. She was an avid reader and possessed more general knowledge than anyone else I ever knew. She read to all her children from the time they were born until they could read on their own. In most cases, this occurred at a pretty early age.

Once she was reading a story about a donkey to me. She reached a point where the donkey was in terrible trouble and, at an extremely sad part, my heart was about to break. I wished this part of the story would come to a rapid end. Suddenly, she was called to the kitchen to rescue something off the woodstove. I knew these stories always had happy endings so to expedite happier times, I quickly moved the book marker ahead, sure that my mother would not notice. Of course, on her return she did notice and realized why. "I'm glad you moved the book marker because this is such a long story. We will continue from here." I was mightily relieved.

My love for reading carried over into the classroom. Sister Alphonsus was always warning me to stop reading such books as *The Rover Boys* and *Henry Ware Fights the Indians*. Thinking I was being clever, I would prop my book inside my big geography text which covered it completely. For a long time Sister thought I was very diligent during study hour.

One day I looked over my shoulder and saw that long dark cloth that led up to Sister's frowning face. "If I catch you one more time, I will confiscate all your books," she declared. She often took them away but gave them back at the end of the day. I was always puzzled at what the word "confiscate" meant.

My next attempt to evade Sister's piercing eyes was to lift up the seat of the desk, crawl under and proceed to read. I was sure she couldn't see me there. Soon I was wrapped up in the tale of how Dick Dare was about to save the girl from the dastardly renegade Simon Gurty. I happened to glance sideways. There was the inevitable long black cloth. I followed it all the way up to Sister's scowling face and this time it seemed for real.

She hauled me up by the back of my shirt. "This is it, Louis. I have had my fill of you. You go home and bring your father back. You cannot return to school until you do."

This was the most catastrophic thing that could have happened to me, to think that I would have to confess to my father that I had been kicked out of school. It was more than I could bear. We all respected our father and admired him so much. He was kind and gentle, and the thought that his son was about to disgrace the whole family called for me to take some kind of drastic action.

Sister Alphonsus had indoctrinated us into the power of prayer. My thought was, if prayer worked, that was the time to try it out. I went into the church that was attached to the school, knelt down at the altar rail and poured my heart out to God. I told him I was sorry that I was such a bad boy. If He would only show me the way, I would reform and be ever so good.

As I left the church, one of the younger nuns came walking by. Wow! An idea came into my head. This was the miracle I was hoping for. I stopped her and told her my dilemma from start to finish. I asked her to intercede with Sister Alphonsus on my behalf. She said she would see what she could do. After what seemed to be a lifetime, Sister Alphonsus appeared. She ruffled my hair and said, "Where did you get all that black hair? Come on, Louis, let's go back into class." My prayer had been instantly answered.

Sister Alphonsus said, "Sister told me about your prayer to God. But don't push your luck. The Lord doesn't always answer prayers as quickly as He did this time."

Of Chipmunks – and a Girl

The nearness to wildlife was a wonderful pleasure for all children in those days and the easiest little animal to catch and tame was a chipmunk. My dog Purp and I had fallen into a system for catching them. The zig-zag split-rail fence that outlined each ranch in Fort Valley ran right in front of our cabin. For their own reasons, chipmunks used the rails of the fence as a highway. As soon as we saw a chipmunk on the rail, we would chase him, Purp on one side of the fence and I on the other. But because of the zig-zag of the fence he had to run twice as far as we did. We would get ahead of him and he would turn and run the other way. Back and forth we went until the chipmunk was worn out, and Purp would reach up and catch him and bring him to me.

A quick glance told me whether to keep him. If he was too big he was a ground chipmunk. I had found out the hard way that a ground chipmunk could bite, but the gentle little tree chipmunk made a lovely pet.

My mother made a little chamois harness with a center snap attached to a long string; the ending tied to a buttonhole of my shirt. The chipmunk soon learned to go into my shirt pocket, grab a pinon nut, and come out and sit on my shoulder to eat it. Sometimes the little fellow would rest in my shirt pocket with just his head peeking out.

We were even allowed to bring our pets to school

on Fridays, providing it didn't disrupt the class. Friday afternoons were special, quiet, relaxed times during which we were supposed to study. Sister occasionally left the room after placing a student monitor in charge.

We kids were seated alphabetically by our last names. Directly in front of me was a girl named Elaine Anderson. She wore her hair in long blond curls and was usually the class monitor during Sister's absence. She took great delight in putting my name down as a violator of the class rules.

I suppose it was distracting for the rest of the class to watch me do tricks with my chipmunk. I would put him in my hand held out at arm's length and release him. He would scamper quickly up my arm and dive into my shirt pocket to reappear instantly with his pinon-nut reward in his front paws. There was a lot of giggling and outright laughter. Of course Elaine wrote my name down as a class disturber.

I had written, "I shall not disturb the class," so many times that I had figured out a system for holding three pencils in my hand and writing three lines at the same time. It isn't easy. Try it. Needless to say, my feeling toward Elaine was not very benevolent.

Once during study period, Elaine relaxed with her head back and her golden curls cascaded onto my desk. I was suddenly filled with an inextinguishable urge to dip a curl into the ink well. I had read about little boys doing such things and I thought it couldn't happen to a more deserving person. My good little guardian angel said, "Don't do it," while the imp on my other shoulder cried, "Go ahead. She deserves it." I moved my hand slowly toward her curl. Holding it gently, I reached toward the ink well. I was concentrating so intently on my dastardly deed that I failed to notice who was approaching from the rear. Whack, came Sister's ruler on my hand. I was back to writing one hundred times, "I shall not disturb the class."

As I grew older, somehow or other my dislike for Elaine changed quite a bit. On many occasions I carried her books all the way to her home. Her folks always had a large box of apples. She would give me one and we would sit and talk over the day's events.

It was very strange how she became prettier and prettier as time went by.

Her folks moved out of town and that was the end of my first romance. I missed her for a long time.

Old Fashioned Right and Wrong

Were the early pioneers who came to Flagstaff different from the people who reside here today? Yes, in many ways. They were no better, no worse, but different.

The clergy was held in high esteem. Our pastor made an effort to visit each parish family at least once a year. We sometimes wondered whether it was a coincidence that he would arrive around supper time. We were always honored and happy when Father came to our house. Mother just put another potato into the pot.

When people were in some kind of trouble they went to their pastor for consolation. There were no professional consultants or advisors. When Father came over to the school playground, the little boys would kneel down and ask for his blessing. At the end of the school year, he handed out report cards to each child. Always, he managed to say something encouraging, no matter what the grades were.

Pastors dressed in a manner that portrayed their position in life, with black suits and stiff, turned-around collars. No one would mistake a minister for the local tennis pro. His dignity was unmistakable.

We had quaint sayings for every occasion. My mother would respond to gossip with, "People who live in glass houses shouldn't throw stones." A practical soul would quote, "A bird in the hand is worth two in the bush." If you stood around the kitchen while your mother was cooking, she might say, "A watched pot never boils."

Some of the boys thought it was great fun to mix up the mottos, thus, "He who laughs last is better than two in the bush."

People halfway believed in some superstitions: breaking a mirror brought seven years of bad luck; never walk under a ladder; a black cat crossing your path at night was a sign of evil.

There was a special, personal guardian angel who looked out for you. He sat on your right shoulder and tried to keep you on the straight and narrow path. He kept you from hitting your head on a rock when you dove into Oak Creek. On your left shoulder was a little imp sent by the devil. He was the one who tried to get you to ditch school and to misbehave in general.

In those days, there was also a thing called "sin." The psychologists had not yet discovered that people do wrong things because they were not properly potty-trained at the right age, or their folks did not treat them kindly, or they had had an unhappy childhood. If someone was a thief or cheated on his spouse, he broke one of the Ten Commandments. These had been given directly to an ancient leader, Moses, by the Lord Himself and they outlined the rules by which people were to live.

There were two kinds of sin, venial and mortal. Venial sin was excusable and trifling. If you went to sleep and slipped off into eternity with a venial sin on your soul and without having asked the Lord's forgiveness, you were safe. But with a mortal sin on your conscience and no repentance, if you died in your sleep, look out – zappo, zippo – down to the bad place you would go.

So, people were very careful to be sorry for their wrongdoings before going to bed, even adding that they wished to be forgiven for the sins they couldn't remember. This always bothered me – as if the Lord didn't know about all the sins you so conveniently forgot to mention.

We were admonished by our families and by the Sisters at school to avoid the occasion of sin. We were not to hang around pool halls where we might learn to gamble and smoke cigarettes. It was best for grown men to stay away from the sinful city of Jerome and, if they were there on business, to leave quickly when they were finished because there was a place in Jerome called the House of Joy where seductive, beautiful women were liable to lure innocent, helpless men to their degradation and downfall.

Many believed that when you died but had not been as good as you could have been, you could not go directly to heaven. You had to spend some time in purgatory. Now, purgatory was not such a bad place. What bothered the people there was that they could look up to heaven and see the folks who had made it, laughing and playing and talking to the Lord just as if they had known him all their lives.

If a relative or friend had died and you thought he had not been as well-behaved as he could have been, probably he was in purgatory. You could reduce his sentence by praying for him. We always finished our prayers at school with a petition for the poor souls in purgatory.

One of the poor souls my mother was sure was in purgatory was my Uncle Harry. Harry was my mother's half brother. Her father, Pius Chambers, born in 1819, died at the age of ninety-two as the result of an accident. He had founded a volunteer fire department during his young manhood and, after retiring, he would occasionally ride on the steam fire engine that furnished the power for the fire hoses. He was not, at his age, supposed to be involved in active firefighting. However, this time the fire was in a theater and he couldn't resist climbing up onto the roof. The roof

Uncle Harry

collapsed and down he came, falling into the aisle. He was rescued by fellow firefighters, but finally succumbed to his injuries.

He had outlived three wives. Each time he married a younger lady and proceeded to have a new family. My mother was the result of his last union. Consequently, she had many half-brothers and half-sisters, some of whom were old enough to be her parents.

In those days many families had a black sheep. Uncle Harry was ours and the subject was hush-hush around polite company. He had passed away when I was still very young, but mother talked about him quite frequently. She was careful to state that Harry had gotten his wild streak from the other side of the family. Harry had left Cincinnati for the Golden West and was prone to hanging around Fisherman's Wharf in San Francisco.

He liked to gamble, play poker, bet on the races and, if the truth were known, probably chase women. We knew for a fact he took a little nip of the sauce once in a while.

One night Harry caught someone cheating at cards and a scuffle occurred. He hit the fellow a little too hard and, being a large strong man, accidentally sent the cheater to his Maker. Poor mother had to endure the horror of it all and the disgrace to the family when Harry had to spend some time in the slammer.

Mother pointed out that Harry was not a bad man but he should have avoided the occasion of sin. So we always said a prayer that Uncle Harry would finally make heaven. I am sure by now that he has made it to the Promised Land. After all, the card player was cheating. But if Uncle Harry is still in purgatory, what a comfort it will be to meet a relative on my way up. Besides, old Harry sounds like my kind of guy.

I have had a little fun here. It was not my intention to belittle those old time beliefs. Most of us still follow them. What a shame that some people in the present society think they did away with sin, because avoiding it sure kept a lot of folks out of trouble.

Flagstaff Christmases Before World War I

Throughout the year the children of the Bader family sort of had Christmas in mind. We were seven – my five older sisters, my special hero and older brother, Dolph, and I, the youngest.

Long before it was time for the tree, we got busy making our own ornaments. For months we had saved colored foil from chocolate candy. Then we acquired a good supply of walnuts, carefully pried the halves apart and took out (and ate) the meats. Then we put

Katherine, the oldest of the family, in Oak Creek Canyon

a looped string between the halves, joined them with a paste made of flour and milk, and wrapped them in the squares of colored foil. They were really very pretty.

To hang on the tree, there were cookies that resembled reindeer and Santas and pieces of home-made taffy. With needles and long threads we made strings of cranberries and popcorn. Some of the pop-corn was tinted with beet juice to make it a nice red. (We always ate the terribly stale popcorn when the tree was finally taken down. Yuck!)

The tree was always a pine. In winter in those days, no roads to the fir or spruce were open.

Do any of you remember the lights for Christmas trees back then? Yes, they were five-inch, twisted, slender, translucent wax candles. They fit into metal holders that fastened like sideways clothespins to the branch tips. Mother and Father placed them carefully so that no flame would be near pine needles.

We hung out stockings on nails along the mantle and we were supposed to go to bed early to give Santa a chance to fill them. The little kids, Dorothy, Jayne and I, got into our nightgowns in front of the glowing fireplace. We used every excuse we could think of to stay up but finally scampered off to the covers. I remember that mother warmed the sheets ahead of time with iron plates from the stove.

After my parents and the older children had de-parted for midnight mass, Dorothy, the oldest of the little kids, would sneak out to feel and shake the packages under the tree, trying to figure out what was inside. Then she would come back to Jayne and me and report her findings.

I always pretty much knew what I would receive.

In the fireplace I had discovered a loose stone and under it a wonderful place to hide my note to Santa Claus. With the help of my sister Jayne, I made a list of the toys I wanted. When no one was looking I would remove the rock, tuck my note into the hole and replace it. I was sure that no one but Santa's Brownies and I knew the secret. In the weeks before Christmas I checked under the stone many times a day and, lo and behold, one day the list would be gone.

On Christmas morning just before the presents were opened, the tree candles were lighted under my parents' careful supervision. They burned only a few minutes, just long enough for us all to sing a couple of verses of Silent Night. These days such a proceeding would turn a fireman's hair white.

Each child received only one toy, usually a pretty one. The other gifts were jackets, underwear and other practical things.

Along the mantle hung the stockings, now bulging strangely. In the toe of each was an orange, a marvelous delicacy in our rather isolated little town. (All the fruit was shipped in by train.) We savored those oranges, pulling the segments apart carefully and even nibbling at the peel.

I always wondered why Santa never brought me everything I asked for, especially the pony. My parents explained that there were many children in the world and gifts had to be shared.

Homemade gifts to each other included cigar boxes of thin cedar wood that could be turned into a sewing box or even a ukulele with rubber bands as strings. There were always wreaths made of seeds and pine cones.

Recently, I happened to go to a meeting at our old house and found it in amazingly good condition. There is a new stove; the hole in the wall where the old stove pipe went through is covered with a metal plate.

Our home in town, the farthest house on San Francisco Street

On it are the words, "God Bless Our Home." This is most appropriate. He certainly did bless it. The five bedrooms and two baths are all newly painted. The stairway and its bannister that I slid down so many times look like new.

Of course, the cookstove is no longer wood-fired. Homemade bread and cinnamon kuchen will not smell quite the same as when our mother had them ready when we came home from school.

Only one change disappointed me. The malpais rocks of the fireplace have been replaced by neat sandstone. I know my secret hiding place is no more. I believe that all fireplaces should have a loose stone so all boys and girls would have a hidey-hole for their notes to Santa. Hopefully, all the fantasies and folk lore that make childhood such a wonderful time will continue on forever. After all, some of us still believe in Brownies and Santa Claus.

The Way It Was During World War I

As we neared entry into the First World War, patriotism ran high. We heard much about the evils of the Crown Prince and the Kaiser. As a young boy I pictured them both as having horns and pointed tails.

Sauerkraut was renamed liberty cabbage. The Katzenjammer Kids (in the colored Sunday funnies) were now called the Shenanigan Kids. Anything with a German name was out.

All the young eligible men hastened to enlist, to join the war to end all wars. Those who did not were labeled slackers. Cartoons depicted a beautiful young girl hanging on the arm of a soldier, glancing disdainfully at a poor fellow in civilian clothes. Jack Dempsey, the great boxer, was vilified because he did not join the armed forces.

One of the first young men to enlist was my brother, Dolph. The war was a whole different affair now that it was so close to home. The Germans were depicted as nonhuman and called the Huns. The thought that my brother would one day be confronted with these hordes was frightening.

The big day to bid farewell to our heroes finally came and the whole town turned out. We were bursting with pride and were sure that our boys would put the enemy in its place.

Some of the girls went off to be Red Cross nurses. My sister Katherine was one of these. Those families who had members in the armed forces placed flags in their windows. On the flag stars were sewn, one for each service person. We had such a flag with two stars proudly hanging in the window of our grocery store on Leroux Street.

One of the places my brother received his training was Palo Alto, California. My mother decided to visit him and to take me along.

It is difficult for this generation to realize that airports did not exist. Lindy had not yet made his famous solo flight; there were no towers where people sat and monitored planes landing and taking off. The mode of transportation was a train with a wheezing, hissing steam engine.

There was much excitement when the train arrived. It was a real event. Folks would go down to the depot to see the train come in, just to have something to do. Children loved to wave to the engineer.

The engine always seemed to me to be something alive. I liked to imagine there was a dragon inside it spewing fire and steam. It was especially exciting now that we were about to enter into the realm of this monster.

After much hugging and kissing from all of the family we boarded the car, assisted by a very courteous redcap. Since it was near evening the berth was made up. I soon entered the "Land of Nod" listening to the comforting click, click of the wheels.

We arrived at our destination, San Francisco, which was as far as the train could take us. Then we had to cross the bay. At that time the Golden Gate

Bridge had not even been thought of, so the crossing was made by ferry boat.

There were only a few seats so most of the passengers were standing. The front of the boat was flat and straight across to expedite landing of the passengers by quick access to the pier. When we were about five feet from the pier and the boat was still moving, the attendant removed the chain across the exit. It was at that moment I saw my brother. Releasing my mother's hand I sprinted past the guard and with a flying jump over the gap, landed in my brother's arms.

My poor mother explained to me later that if I had not made it I could have fallen into the sea and possibly could have been crushed by the boat.

It was the first time this little Arizona boy had seen California poppies - so he brought a bouquet for his mother

The next trial I handed my mother, while riding the cable car, did not help her much either. We were sitting on the side of the car when a gust of wind came up and my hat flew off. Without hesitation, I jumped off to recover it. There was a lot of bell-clanking and screeching of brakes, but I got my hat and jumped back on the cable car before it had come to a complete stop. The conductor pleaded with my mother to please control her little boy. Needless to say, I received another lecture.

John Jakle
Killed in action in World War II, a full colonel.

While waiting near Fisherman's Wharf, I spied a large sea lion sunning himself. Running over, I sat down on his back shouting, "Gittee-up." He growled like a dog and snapped at me while my mother frantically ran over and grabbed me. Thinking back, it must have been quite a day for my mother. I remember that people spoke of her as being prematurely grey. I wonder why.

After a very short visit with my brother, we returned to Flagstaff. Everyone was raising Victory Gardens, hogs, chickens, and anything else that might help the war effort.

Occasionally, troop trains would pass through the town. Everyone would go to the station loaded down with cakes, cookies, cigarettes, books, and a lot of homemade things for the soldiers. The stops were all too short. A couple of times my brother was one of the soldiers passing through. It was such a brief moment, treasured by all, but sad when we watched the train disappear.

Our next notice of the whereabouts of the troops was from France. My brother and his outfit had landed in Brest, but by this time the war was winding down. None of our boys, as they were known, saw any action. That was the phraseology for not being in any battles. However, we were still proud of them and thought of all of them as heroes.

It was a great day when, on November eleventh, 1918, armistice was declared. There was no snow on the ground. My friend John Jakle and I got cow bells and ran through our small town ringing them as loud as we could shouting, "Armistice, armistice." We did not really know the meaning of the word, only that the war was over.

John said he was happy that Dolph could come home and that there would not be any more wars. We were really convinced that this was the war to end all wars. Was that not what all the grown-ups had told us?

Little did we suspect then that John would get an appointment to West Point, achieve the highest rank and give his life for his country.

Being as serious as only little boys can be, we promised when we parted that we would always be each other's best friend. I have always held this dear to my heart. To this day, I believe that the highest honor I will ever receive is to have been John Jakle's best friend.

To the Grand Canyon, 1918-Style

Today, it is an easy one-and-a-half hour trip from Baderville to the Grand Canyon. This was not so many years ago. In those days it was a real tour. I remember my mother's packing and making preparations for herself and my father to embark on an exciting journey for their time – Flagstaff to the Grand Canyon.

When the day for departure came, all seven kids and my folks headed for the old Bank Hotel. The girls were in the back of our Model-T pickup; Mom and Pop were in the front seat; my brother, Dolph, and I were riding our horses, and our dog, Purp, was trailing the whole entourage. We arrived at the hotel without incident except for a few dogs barking at and threatening Purp.

At that time, the Bank Hotel was the swankiest place in town, with a bank downstairs and hotel rooms in the upper story. Many a glittering social event was held there with lovely Mamie Fleming, daughter of pioneer Tom McMillan, as the hostess. This building is still in existence and has become a historical monument. It is located directly across the street from the Amtrak station. Look up at the top corner and you will see carved in stone "BANK HOTEL."

The stage, with the horses hitched up, was waiting in front of the hotel. The folks who were brave enough to take this arduous trip climbed up to the extremely hard seats carrying their cushions and pillows. There was laughing and good-natured kidding among the men, while the ladies were more reserved. The driver and his helper put all the luggage aboard. There was more waving, hugging and kissing of relatives, children and friends. After all, this was a big deal – they would be gone at least a week. They would change horses first at Fern Mountain and at intervals thereafter, all the way.

A younger Lou at the Grand Canyon

Since my brother was the only one besides Dad who could drive the Tin Lizzie, he drove it home with all my sisters on board, slowly, since his horse was tied behind.

But I was allowed to follow the stage out of town on my horse. When my folks motioned me to go back I felt deserted and thought, "This is how it must feel to be an orphan."

Time passes fast, especially when you have five big sisters to comfort you. Soon my folks were home again, tired and a little worn, but with many a fine tale to tell. My Dad was a wonderful raconteur and we all relived their experiences and delighted in the pictures he had taken with his very large box camera.

The Canyon has always held great fascination. Recently my wife Emma Jean and two of her daughters, Jeanie Hansen and Mary Simpson, walked from the North Rim across the canyon and up – the South Rim. I would have gone with them but you know how it is – girls walk so slowly.

The Bank Hotel

Entertainment

Mostly, folks provided their own entertainment, such as dances, parties and card tournaments. However, we did have a movie theater close enough to walk to in the evening. It was, and still is, called the Orpheum.

The movies were, of course, silent. The action was accompanied by a piano player named Billy Costigan who, we were told, had migrated to Arizona for his health. It was whispered that he had consumption, another word for tuberculosis. A good many early settlers came to Flagstaff expecting to die soon and lived to a ripe old age. Costigan's skill was magnificent, a real contribution to our enjoyment of the movie. When the villain was about to escape or there was a fight, his music would crescendo to a wonderful fortissimo that shook the rafters. During matinees, the children augmented the excitement by stamping their feet.

The Saturday afternoon program included a serial, which always ended in the middle of an impossible situation, making it mandatory to see the next episode the following week.

All the schools made use of the Orpheum's large stage for plays and skits. Under the guidance of teachers, many an extravaganza was produced. Long suffering and patient mothers designed and sewed elaborate costumes for the children. A large and enthusiastic crowd applauded with great vigor each time a child sang a song in a squeaky voice or a pretty little girl pirouetted in her tutu.

A big attraction was the Chautauqua, a traveling "educational" institution that performed in a tent. For the local folk, it was a great treat to see many of the wonderful plays of the day performed by professional actors. There were lectures and concerts and the very popular blackface minstrels. There was many a belly laugh at the antics of Mr. Bones and Mr. Interlocutor.

There was an afternoon and an evening performance – the afternoon for children and young people. I managed to come early, crawl under the tent and sit in the bleachers, trying to be invisible. At the same time the help were bringing in props and the actors were rehearsing. Of course they saw me, but now I am sure they were glad to have another warm body present. They had handed out passes to anyone who would distribute them, as afternoons were always a poor house.

The group of performers remained in Flagstaff until they exhausted their repertoire. We were always sorry to see them pull down their tent and leave town.

When the Circus Came to Town

Posters in garish colors went up all over town, the advance publicity of the circus. Little kids gawked at the sight of a beautiful lady with her head stuck in the mouth of a ferocious lion or breathed in awe at the graceful trapeze artists in tights, catching each other in midair.

When the circus arrived on a special train, every living soul who could get away scurried to the depot to see the animals and wagons disembark.

First came the elephants, each with a handler who held a cane-like stick with a sharp pointed barb on the end. It was called an elephant hook and the handler did not hesitate to use it. I got upset whenever he struck his charge because I could see small chunks of hide removed and the pink color of flesh revealed underneath.

With all the paraphernalia off the train, a parade was organized. What a thrill! Ornate red and gilt wagons pulled by horses with plumes on their heads were followed by gaudy cages in which lions and tigers paced back and forth.

At the end came a most splendid sight, a wagon encrusted with jewels and gold, bearing a steam calliope. The shrill, wheezing notes could be heard for many blocks.

One of the exciting attention-getting stunts was

the ascension of a man in a balloon. A large ring was connected to the bottom of the balloon. Several men held it and more men held ropes attached to the balloon itself. Under the ring they started a very hot fire of pitch logs that had been sprinkled with kerosene. In a dangerous spot as near the fire as possible was, of course, my little self.

One of the men got too close to the fire and a very large blister arose on his leg. He let out a curse word, took a knife out of his pocket, pulled up his pant leg and stuck the blister which immediately collapsed. I was flabbergasted. To me it seemed that he had cut something off his leg.

As the hot air filled the balloon, it became a struggle for the men on the ropes to hold it. They maneuvered it away from the fire and attached a large gondola basket underneath. The balloonist stepped in and away he went. Where he landed is a mystery to me, even to this day.

Watching the tents being erected held the children spellbound. Picture three men alternately hitting a stake in perfect rhythm as they pounded it into the hard Flagstaff ground. Fascinating!

We were always surprised to see the cooperation of the elephants as the tents went up. On command, they grabbed ropes with their trunks and easily pulled great sheets of canvas into place.

Some men busily put up booths called side shows, fronted by vivid paintings on huge canvases of what would be going on inside. They extolled the wonders of the two-headed calf, the bearded lady, the world's fattest girl and many other oddities. We were invited to witness the most horrible creature in the world. One glimpse would make strong men pale and women faint.

Further along were pictures of scantily clad females and a big sign stating that the dance they did would drive men wild. "Ladies, do not let your husbands attend. You may never see them again," the barker called out.

After the tents were up, large wagons of sawdust arrived from the local lumber mill. Some of the town boys were employed to spread it around in the show rings used for acrobats and for animal tricks.

At the evening performance it looked like the whole town was there. Every seat was filled.

Here came the ringmaster, elegantly attired. In his wonderful sonorous voice he called out, "Ladies and gentlemen, boys and girls," and the show began.

The clowns were a special treat. We kids thought the tricks they did were truly hilarious. We ate Crackerjacks and hot dogs and went home feeling we had had a really good time.

Television will never take the place of the smell and sights, the total excitement of a real live circus.

Delivering Groceries

All of the grocery stores maintained a delivery service. Early in the morning, the grocer phoned each of his regular customers to get the daily order from the housewife. A delivery boy brought the brown paper sacks to the door. The family was billed once a month. A wonderful service this was, especially during the winter.

My father was a keen advocate of delivery. He thought it best to keep some of the shoppers out of the vegetable department and expressed his views quite often at supper. He had a special name for some of the women who poked their fingers into soft fruit or tomatoes. He called them old biddies, although he remained at all times courteous and pleasant while on the job.

Our grocery store delivery truck was a Model-T Ford, a real honest-to-goodness pickup. It had to be cranked by hand, a rather dangerous, risky procedure. You had to grab the handle, push in to engage the engine, pull up quickly time and time again. The diabolic contraption was supposed to release whenever the engine fired up. Unfortunately, it did not always work. Many times the crank handle caught and flipped back, landing a mighty smack on the wrist of the poor cranker.

Someone with his arm in a sling was not an uncommon sight. We could almost always guess what had happened to him. Just imagine, Henry Ford didn't even have a sign on his invention stating, "Cranking this machine could be dangerous to your health." My, my, wouldn't his liability insurance be high today?

Since I had five pretty sisters, the young delivery boy was always glad to come to our house.

Integrity

I am sure that there are as many honest people in today's world as there were in the past, but among the homesteaders in early Flagstaff, goodwill and integrity no doubt reached an all-time high. A man's word was his bond, a binding force that needed no written documents. No lawyers or title companies were involved; just a handshake would consummate a bargain.

A prevalent way of doing business was grubstaking. One party furnished seed, groceries and sundries to the rancher who did the work. They agreed to split the profits at the end of the season.

My father, as the proprietor of a general grocery store, made many of these transactions. On one occasion, George Cutler, a Doney Park rancher, grubstaked and fell upon hard times. The bean crop did not pan out. Not only was there no profit but also there was a loss. Without any hesitation, father agreed to advance seed and food for another year.

The new season was entirely different. The rain was bountiful and all the dry-farmers were in seventh heaven. One evening while we were all at supper (that's what the evening meal was called in those days) there was a knock at the door. My father opened it and said, "Hello, George, come on in. Sit down and have supper with us."

After supper my sister Pearl played the piano. My

brother Dolph scratched at his violin. We all knew he would never make the Philharmonic, but his efforts were appreciated. I sang "Old Dog Tray." My mother provided home-made doughnuts and coffee, with hot chocolate for the kids.

George got up, thanked us for a nice evening and handed my father an envelope. He said, "Here is your

Adolph G. Bader, Sr. on Rattler

half, Ad. Last year was bum, but we had a good one this time." My father took the envelope and without looking inside said, "Thanks." They shook hands. As George was about to go out the door he turned and said, "The same deal next year, Ad?" My dad said, "Sure."

This was an ideal way of doing business. Unfortunately, in some of the years that followed, unscrupulous people who did not honor their debts or verbal agreements moved into the area. But the old-timers who know each other continue to do business in the same manner, even to this day.

Winter in Flagstaff

Long before anyone heard of BTUs (British Thermal Units) or insulation factors, Flagstaff families tried to keep warm in winter with wood and coal. Some folks had managed to put sawdust or cinders in the house walls between the studs, but most houses were not insulated at all.

The main source of heat was the kitchen stove. Since three meals a day were cooked on it, this fire was seldom out. On Saturday nights, we set a big round galvanized tub a foot or two in front of the opened oven, half filled it with water from the tap and warmed it with boiling water from the ever-present kettle. Kids were scrubbed in rotation.

Of course there were no heat tapes for water pipes and most pipes were frozen a good deal of the time. We found out that running water does freeze. Mama made coffee quite often from melted snow.

Clothes left out on the line overnight were as stiff as concrete in the morning. If by accident water was left in the washtub on the back porch, an ice pick was needed to remove it. The boiling water from the kettle was forever being poured into the sink to open the frozen pipes. Milk was delivered to our step in glass quart bottles topped with rounds of waxed cardboard. The cream rose to the top and then peeked up out of its little trap door.

We little kids in bed had quilts piled so high on

us that we almost had to holler for help to turn over. By morning the heat irons placed in the bed might have slipped out of the towels they were wrapped in and it would practically freeze your toes if you accidentally touched one.

Winter in Flagstaff

My father, bless him, started a fire in the fireplace early in the morning. Still, it was like a death march to scramble from the bedroom to the livingroom warmth. We stood so close we would almost fry our eyelashes, then quickly turned to toast our rear ends. We dressed for school right there by the heat.

After-school arrivals saw socks, mittens and even underwear hanging from the mantle, giving off steam. Mittens, of course, were attached in pairs by a long crocheted string. You threaded a mitten up one coat sleeve and down the other. This way, our folks optimistically believed, you couldn't lose them.

No one cleared the residential streets; there was no school bus. Everyone walked to school. The older children did the trail-breaking with the young kids following in their footsteps. If things were too bad, we turned for home. Any missed school work had to be made up later.

As soon as they could, after a snowfall, folks got out to shovel the flakes off the boardwalks. These were constructed of full-dimension two-by-twelves and held up for many a year. Downtown, the merchants or their clerks quickly cleared off the walks and freed up the entrances to their stores.

On downtown streets, teams of horses pulled along fresno scrapers, followed on foot by shouting teamsters. Soon everything was back to normal.

People read a lot in the winter. There was no radio, no TV. This part of the year seemed to stretch into eternity. Then one day when you stepped out into the yard, instead of frozen ground there was mud, wonderful mud. Nothing was more welcome than mud except the flash of blue from the wing of a mountain bird. They would come around to reconnoiter, to check things out. Even when they disappeared again, we were sure that spring wasn't far away.

Soon they were back. That flash of blue looked like a piece of the sky. The blue birds were joined by calling meadowlarks. Snow birds left, to be replaced by chickadees. The aspen trees decided to release their buds to show soft chartreuse. Pretty soon wildflowers started pushing up between green grass blades and we knew we had made it. We had managed to survive. Our only thought on seeing the new wonder and beauty of the birth of spring was that it had all been worthwhile.

We Leave Flagstaff

There came a day when our family had to move on and leave the area I loved so much. It was for the same reason that had brought us to Flagstaff – my father's health. The change of climate from Cincinnati to the pure mountain air of Arizona had helped his bad case of asthma only temporarily. Now the doctors were suggesting a hot, dry climate such as there was in where else but Needles, California.

I left Flagstaff on the Santa Fe train in the charge of my oldest sister, Katherine. We arrived at the Fred Harvey Hotel in Needles and stepped off into a completely different world. There were palm trees and a great extent of lawn. Hundreds of birds fluttered about. I saw a man walking around with a long stick in his hand. On the end of the stick was a pointed nail and he punched pieces of paper and other debris and put them in a bag. I thought, "What a wonderful job. I hope one day when I grow up, I can have such a marvelous occupation. It would be wonderful to be able to be in such a nice park and around all those beautiful birds." My ecstatic opinion of the place soon evaporated.

My happy high feeling soon became a great downfall. When we left the park we encountered nothing but sand and greasewood. The houses and the stores were all run down. Compared with Flagstaff, I thought it was the ugliest town in the world.

My father had rented a house next door to the mortuary. My bedroom was the screen porch. There was a side yard of three feet between my cot and the funeral parlor. My anxiety was not lowered by the tales some of the neighbor boys told. They spoke graphically about how the spirits of the dead next door were known to roam at night. I should listen for strange noises. Many a night I slept with my head under the covers. I wished for my dog, Purp, who had been left behind because he was off on one of his jaunts when the family left in the Tin Lizzie. I was to get him back later.

It was a happy day when we moved to a new house that my father had constructed. Behind this house was a small church. The congregation was black and I learned they were Holy Rollers.

The tales of their gyrations piqued my curiosity. I was determined to see for myself. One Sunday afternoon I sneaked into the church and sat myself down in the furthermost pew. I was doing my invisible act, hoping no one would see me. Soon the congregation began to assemble. No one paid any attention to me. I was positive now that if I didn't squirm I would remain undiscovered.

The preacher entered wearing a much-too-large black gown. As he walked back and forth it swept the floor. The bottom edges were covered with needles and other trash. The switching and gliding of his gown only added to the dramatics of his gestures as he worked himself up to a peak of religious fervor. People approached the front of the church making weird noises and speaking in a strange language. Some fell to the floor and actually did roll around. Soon everything was as lively as a hoe-down festival. I reckoned I should get out of there while the getting was good.

Scurrying out, I practiced rolling my eyes and jerking and mumbling, as I tried to imitate what I had witnessed in the church. I had always delighted in scaring and teasing my five older sisters and this was to be my last triumph. A startled lady saw me on the street, shook her head and walked over to me. "You poor boy. Can I help?" I just mumbled some incoherent gibberish and walked off, jerking as wildly as I could, leaving her standing with her mouth agape.

That evening while the whole family was seated in the front room, reading or doing homework, I thought I would try out my new act. Falling to the floor, I started to jerk and kick, mumbling the strange language I had practiced. My father said, "Good Lord, the boy's having a fit."

"No he isn't," my sister Jayne declared. "He has been to the black church behind us. I saw him sneak in Sunday afternoon."

Yanking me to my feet, my mother proceeded to lecture me on what could happen to a little Catholic boy who attended other churches. I promised not to be involved in such a ceremony again, but I thought that the people of that church were sure having a lot of fun.

The boys attending the grammar school were a new breed to me. They were tough and ready for a fight and especially had an aversion to a new boy. They constantly challenged me with taunts and insults about Flagstaff.

I finally reached the end of my endurance and challenged one particularly vocal boy to a fight. I declared I could lick him any day. I would show them how those of us from Flagstaff could fight. This was met with much scorn, hooting and cat calls.

The protocol of a fight in my country was to approach your opponent with a real wood chip on your shoulder and demand, "Knock that off." If the fight was on, your adversary would send the chip flying. Much to my surprise, the boy dispensed with the chip routine and hit me first.

Fists were soon flying fast and furious. Neither one of us was aware of the approach of a teacher. She warned us that if we did that again we would be sent to the principal. This was the greatest threat she could make, as the principal was a formidable man who had a very thick and heavy yardstick and was known to use it.

Lou and his new best friend
Needles, California

When the teacher took her leave, I couldn't resist saying, "Good thing she came to save you. I had you going. You were really licked."

"That's right," he admitted, "but I can lick you wrestling."

That was all we needed and we were at it again, rolling around in the desert sand. Just when I had managed to get a scissors grip with my legs around his waist, squeezing hard and just when his eyes were about to pop out of his head, around the corner came a grown up. Who else was it but the teacher.

We didn't talk to each other as we slowly walked to the principal's office. We were two frightened little boys. We sat for a while in an outer office, contemplating the dire consequences of our misbehavior, probably the teacher's recommendation that we be beaten within an inch of our lives.

When we were summoned to the principal's office, we saw an extremely large man who said nothing, just sat there and looked at us menacingly. Reaching up, he removed a large thick yardstick from the wall. Waving it in our faces, he said, "Now, what's this all about?"

I was so impressed by the stick and this very large man, I was tongue-tied. But the other kid managed to spit it out, "He said he could lick me."

The principal asked, "Did he lick you?"

"Yes."

Putting the stick back on the wall, much to our relief, he said, "Well, now that this is all settled, I want you two boys to be friends. Shake hands and go back to class."

There were two happy boys who walked back to

class. And now I had another best friend; that's what he became the rest of the time we spent in Needles, California.

With him, I explored the river and a boggy area called the slue. Before I left, I had learned to love the desert and could see its beauty, even though it was different from my beloved ranch and the San Francisco Peaks.

Purp

It must have been around 1917 in Flagstaff when one summer afternoon I was paging through a photo album of our family's Cincinnati days. Here was a picture of a little child and a large dog. In answer to my questions, Mother told me the little one in the dress was myself and the dog was a collie named Bruce. Instantly, I had to know what happened to Bruce and why he wasn't with us in Arizona. She told me that he

Beloved Purp
The bravest little dog

had stayed in Cincinnati with a cousin of ours because it was difficult to transport him by train. She assured me that he was well and happy with his new family and that we all missed him.

Then and there the desire to have a dog of my own awakened in me, especially to have one as large and beautiful as Bruce. I constantly put out hints and overtures to my brother, sisters and parents that every little boy should have a dog. Suppose a bear or a mountain lion should attack? I would have to be protected by a big, brave dog, very much like Bruce in the picture.

Finally, one evening after supper my dad said, "I have something for you," as he walked out to the back porch. My thoughts flew – this is my lucky day – a big beautiful collie is to be mine.

My father returned, holding a small black and white puppy. I knew instinctively that this was no collie and my disappointment showed clearly on my face. Dad assured me he was find breed, a wire-haired fox terrier and terriers were very brave.

I could only blurt, "What happened to his tail?" Dad explained it was the custom to dock the tail of this kind of dog.

Reluctantly I took him in my arms and he reached up and gave me a kiss. This little fellow seemed to know he had to make good in a hurry. He didn't lick me, he basted me. From that moment on, he was my dog. A genuine and complete affection existed between us. This little puppy had an impact on my life that guided my whole attitude toward animals. Purp and I were inseparable and I was sure he was a ten-times better dog than some old collie.

He slept on my bed. When we were at the table he sat on the floor beside me and looked up longingly, hoping I would slip him a morsel or two. Dad frowned on that practice, but I always managed slyly to hand him a crust or a bone.

We spent many an hour in the woods. Purp would come home exhausted, having dug into every prairie dog hole he came across. He was the one who taught me how to catch chipmunks on the split- rail fence.

He had a vendetta against porcupines and, of course, always came out second best. We both suffered agonies when he had to have implanted quills pulled from his face.

He never learned to avoid conflict. I was always on the alert to keep him away from other male dogs, no matter what size. He once got into a tangle with a large Airedale and it was only my intervention that saved him from serious injury. He had the heart of a lion and the courage of his convictions.

Our back yard in town had a fence with a nice rail along the top. We would race along the rail, pretending it was a tightrope. With this set-up, all the neighborhood children would play a great game with Purp. We would run from one side of the yard to the other, back and forth, then jump to the top rail, trying to escape the mock ferocity of Purp. He was always careful not to hurt anyone he caught, so we had the vicarious thrill of being attacked by a "vicious animal" with the assurance that there really was no danger.

When Purp was almost full-grown we began to notice some dead chickens around with obvious signs that they had been mauled. Since Purp was the only animal who had access to the chicken yard, suspicion fell on him. I made every effort to throw the blame on a raccoon or a skunk –but to no avail because one day he was caught in the act.

The decision from on high was that he was to be broken of this habit right now or he would have to go. I was devastated at the thought of losing my pal. Immediately I consulted my friend, Fuller. He said, "When you catch him in the act, you tie him up and hit him with the chicken."

I hated everything about that idea, but I was desperate and knew I had to do it. Some time later I did catch him in the act. I scolded him as vigorously as I could, tied him to a tree and hit him time and time again with the chicken, feeling sick and praying the whole time that the message would get through to him.

It did. Purp learned his lesson and from then on could be trusted around hens and even little chicks. I was in debt again to Fuller for his practical folklore.

When my oldest sister, Katherine, and I departed by train for Needles, California, Purp was off on one of his periodical absences. I didn't get a chance to bid him good-bye, but my folks promised they would bring him with them when they followed in the Tin Lizzie. I was extremely disappointed when they arrived without him.

My father tried to explain to me that male dogs were prone to wander off at certain seasons. He would contact a truck driver in Flagstaff and have him bring Purp the next time he came to Needles. He would arrange with Mrs. Laura Runke, the lady who had purchased our house, to feed him until that time.

Day after day I waited. One afternoon after school, there he was. Never was there a happier kid or dog. Purp was so excited he ran around in circles emitting little cries of joy. I had a time slowing him down so I could hug him. Finally, when I did get hold of him, he smothered me with wet kisses.

Now we were in a whole different atmosphere. The Colorado River had not been harnessed. There were sloughs and swamplands to explore, new wildlife like ducks and mud hens, muskrats and beavers to discover. I am sure Purp thought he had died and gone to heaven. We spent many happy hours down by the river. The river bed would change almost daily. Sometimes in the spring with the winter run-off, there was great fear that it would come up into the town, but by the next week it could be half a mile away.

The water was the color of red mud, though it was referred to as the Golden Colorado. A glass of it, allowed to settle for a few minutes, would have an inch of mud in the bottom. For drinking water it had to have special treatment and the taste was terrible, especially for folks used to pure melted snow filtered by cinders at the ranch.

There were fantastic pieces of driftwood and pools with all kinds of insects, polliwogs and frogs, wherever the river temporarily abandoned its bed. It was down by the river I first fired a friend's 12-gauge shotgun. It promptly knocked me flat on my back.

When school days began, Purp was kept penned up in the back yard. He didn't take kindly to that or accustom himself to waiting for me after school. Instead he spent his days becoming an expert at tunneling under the fence. Invariably he would be waiting at the front steps, wagging his stumpy tail and jumping up on me with wet kisses. It required such constant vigilance to keep Purp from liberating himself from the yard that we finally became resigned to letting him roam just like the other dogs in the small town. Of course there was no leash law. He promptly took advantage of this freedom and would be gone four and five days at a time, as in the old days at the ranch.

With my little-boy mentality, I remembered how I had punished Purp when he destroyed the chickens and how well it had worked. I resolved that the next time he came home from one of his sojourns to the river swamps, I would punish him. Then he would learn he had done something wrong and would mend his ways.

He had been gone again and one day after school there he was, wagging his stubby tail and rushing up to greet me, full of love and happiness. I took a stern posture and said, "Purp, you bad dog," and reached out and hit him. He glanced up with a startled look and turned and left. I ran after him calling, "Purp, come back. I didn't mean to hit you." But he turned the corner and was gone. I never saw him again.

For weeks I searched, my heart like lead. I was sure he had gone because I had hit him. My father tried to console me. He knew Purp would never leave voluntarily. Perhaps the Mojave Indians had gone off with him. Now I know that animals hold no grudges. Something surely happened to Purp in the precarious life he led.

If dogs have a spirit, and I'm sure they do, one day Purp and I will be together again. We will catch chipmunks and have tame prairie dogs and track mountain lions. He will forgive me for hitting him and he will lick my face and baste me all over again.

Moving On

After a time in Needles, the doctors thought a climate with more moisture was just the thing for my dad's health. So we were off to Los Angeles.

True to pattern, my dad went off first, leaving my less-than-five-foot-tall mother to sell the house, ship the furniture, bundle up the kids and follow later.

Before leaving, Dad purchased a new Model-T Ford touring car for our transportation to Los Angeles. Packing food, water and everything else we could crowd into it, we took off along unpaved Highway 66. Unpolluted Los Angeles was a garden spot in those days.

Years passed, and one day I could see my way back to Flagstaff and the ranch. All my obligations were fulfilled. Many living experiences had piled up, many happy, a few sad.

Things hadn't changed much. The old cabin had completely disappeared, but the grass and the wild flowers were the same.

For years now, I have enjoyed all this and feel lucky that I can spend my golden years where I spent my boyhood.

I even had time to attend Northern Arizona University where I learned to cast bronze, and with my lovely wife Emma Jean, I'm sure I can add, "They lived happily ever after."

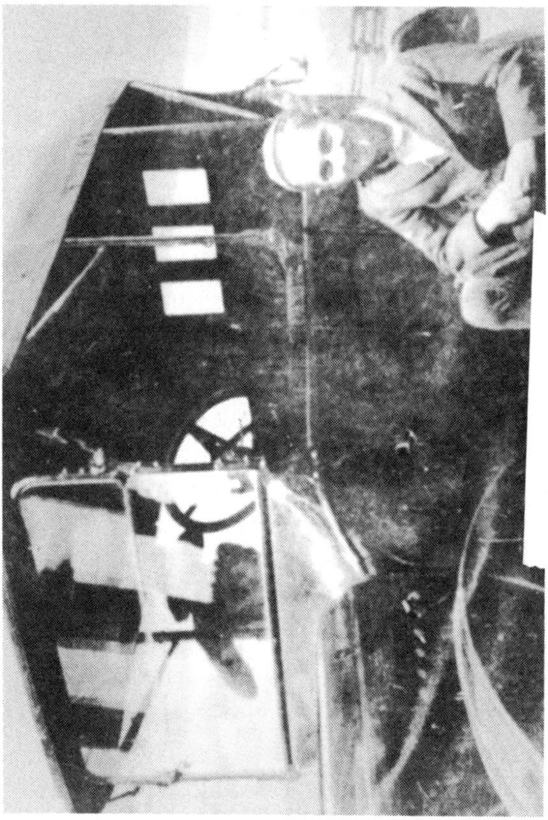

The wonderful new Tin Lizzie, our transportation to California on the dirt Highway 66

Note

I can't wind these yarns down without telling you about a couple of good friends we met after returning to the ranch.

Nino

I admit that until recently I have been a closet animal-talker. I know that it is perfectly all right to talk to your dog. Everybody does that. You tell him, "There you are. How did you get all those porcupine quills in your face?" You half expect the dog to reply, "I was sniffing around this little animal and he hit me in the kisser with his tail." Or, "You dumb dog, don't you know you must go outside to do that?" This is acceptable.

But I must confess, every time I went out and talked to one of my baby doves, I looked around to see if anyone was listening. I would say to a little creature no bigger than my thumb, "My, you're getting big. It's a good thing we didn't see you around Thanksgiving or we might have thought you were a turkey." Then I would quickly look over my shoulder to make sure no men in white coats were approaching to haul me off to the funny farm.

But now things are different. My granddaughter, Cosette, is taking her master's degree in psychology at Berkeley and she tells me it is all right to talk to animals. Boy, what a relief! Now I can brazenly speak out any time I wish. Which brings me to Nino, my donkey, the animal I talk to every day.

Before I can tell you about Nino, I must tell you about Misty, his mother. About twenty-five years ago,

I met a casual acquaintance in the line at the market. Actually, it was in a bar. He found himself a little short of money and put the touch on me for twenty dollars. "Lou, I will give you my donkey for security." I assured him, "Please don't do that. I already have twelve free-loaders. Don't do me any favors. I trust you. Don't give me your donkey." However, next morning out in my field was a light tan burro. I never laid eyes on the donkey mortgager again.

I called the animal inspector to look Misty over and he was amazed. He said, "This animal must be forty years old. There are brands on her made by the Army and the Army hasn't used burros for forty years. We quickly learned to love Misty. The children used to sit on her, but she would never move unless someone led her.

One spring morning twenty-one years ago we awoke to a startling sight. There beside Misty was the cutest little burro in all the world. It was short-coupled, power-puff soft, with saucer eyes, and tiny black hoofs – exactly like a Mexican cartoon of a baby burro. Now there was some question about his father, since no one knew of a male burro in the whole valley. We could only come to the conclusion that it was the first virgin birth in all of donkeydom. We didn't think it nice to call him a bastard.

Not long afterwards, Misty went to the great white burro heaven in the sky and Nino was devastated. I began to console him by talking to him, putting my arms around him and whispering in his ear. This became a daily custom.

Every morning when I go out to feed the horses, Nino starts to whine. I know exactly what he is saying.

"You like the horses better than you do me." I reply, "No, I don't. You know that you're just as good as anyone else around here." He answers, "I don't believe that. I don't even think you are going to give me anything to eat. Look at me; I'm wasting away." Then I go over and talk to him. I praise his beautiful ears and his melodious voice. After a while he begins to believe me and starts to eat.

Sometimes in the spring when the grass is green, I keep the animals in during the day to keep the old horses from eating too much. When I let them out and am standing at the gate, the horses pass me up like a dirty shirt. But not Nino. He comes up to me and we have a conversation. He talks back with a kind of wheezing noise and keeps it up as long as I will stand there.

Nino is very gregarious and loves to visit the neighbors' horses, especially in the summer. He goes over the fences as if they weren't there and he stays for weeks. But he always knows how to come home when times get tough. Then it's always the same, as if he had

Nino

never left home, and the same old talking ritual starts all over again.

Recently, a friend was talking to me about Nino. "What do you do with that burro?"

I replied, "Oh, lots of things."

"Just what? Has he ever had a saddle on him?"

"Well, no, not exactly."

"Burros are supposed to be pack animals. Has he ever had a pack on his back?"

"Well, no."

"Doesn't he constantly jump the fence? Didn't you and a couple of helpers have to raise the fence a foot to keep him in?"

"Yes."

"Has he ever done a day's work in his life?"

"No, but – "

"Well, why do you buy hay and pamper a no-good bum of a burro? What good is he?"

"Well, I – I go out every morning and put my arms around him, and I hug him."

Junior

When I first saw Junior he was huddled in the corner of the Humane Society office, a pitiful little mass of skin and bones. His white and burnt sienna hide seemed to glitter and his great big brown eyes appeared too large for such a small animal.

As president of the society I was making one of my routine visits. I inquired of the director, "What's that little cow doing here?"

"That's not a cow, but a little bull. The dairies dispose of their surplus bull calves, giving them to anyone who will take them. This one proved too much for somebody so they brought him out here."

"What are you going to do?" I asked.

"I don't know," he replied. "If someone doesn't take him today I will just have to put him to sleep."

I looked over at him and thought, "Oh, no you don't." Walking over I picked him up, carried him out and set him down beside me in my pickup.

I said, "Little fellow, I don't know what I am going to do with you, but I will give it a good try."

The first stop was a visit to the supply shop. Fortunately, I was able to obtain a bucket with a large nipple protruding from the side, but no supplement to mix with the powdered milk. My thoughts: What could I substitute? Why not Pablum? If that was good enough for human babies, why not little bulls?

When I got the little critter home I set him up by

a wood stove and proceeded to mix up my concoction. I poked the nipple at him, but got no response. Dipping my fingers into the mixture, I wiped it across his muzzle. He licked at it and I then shoved the nipple home. The poor little half-starved calf guzzled the milk so fast I had to slow him up by pulling it out occasionally. He looked up at me. It was then that he considered me for all time to be his mother. Therefore, the name, Junior.

Junior grew by leaps and bounds. The first traumatic event was the removal of his horns. When they began to show, the vet, with plenty of anaesthetic, nipped them in the bud. The only one it bothered much was me. Junior came through the operation like a little trooper.

At that time I was building a new barn. This gave the little bull plenty of time to spend with me, and that he did. I could not turn around without stepping on him. He was always sticking his wet nose into my hand, looking for some goodies.

By this time he was growing like a weed and did he grow! He grew and grew. Because of his size it was very difficult to keep him in a stall. Just by leaning on the gate he would make it groan. Even the side of the barn was not safe.

It was a strange sight indeed to see this large animal following me around like a puppy. But it was a relationship that we both enjoyed. I drew the line whenever he tried to enter the house with me. But sure enough there he would be, waiting for me, expecting a handout, whenever I came out of the house again.

Finally, there came a day when Junior noticed the cows in the field adjoining the barn. Since he had been reared with horses, I am sure he was surprised and eager to join creatures that resembled himself. So over or through the fence he went. This of course was met with great displeasure by the owner of the purebred Herefords, although I thought that Junior, a purebred Guernsey, might add a little bit of class.

I sympathized with the owner of the Herefords and promised to do something to keep Junior in, but to no avail. He was constantly in the neighbor's field. However, every time I would go to bring him home, he would do a little dance of joy and follow me obediently.

What to do with Junior? There were several suggestions from practical folks like, "Why don't you make roasts and steaks out of him?" This thought was extremely repugnant to me. One just does not eat his adopted children. It smacks of cannibalism.

I knew I had to solve this problem when Junior went to visit another neighbor. This person became hysterical and came at me like a mad man. I am sure he thought Junior was somehow going to gore him to his death. The gentle creature would have made Ferdinand the flower-smelling bull look like Qaddafi.

About this time a rancher from New Mexico, while delivering hay to my barn, noticed Junior. He remarked what a beautiful animal he was. Would I consider selling him? He owned twenty young heifers and needed a bull for crossbreeding.

The decision had to be made immediately. I knew I had to let Junior go to solve the problem of my uninformed neighbors who did not understand this gentle animal, and probably never should have come to the country. I hated to lose my friend but the practical side of me overcame my misery.

The farmer, sensing my feelings, consoled me by describing the paradise that Junior would enjoy. He painted a word picture of Junior grazing in an apple orchard surrounded by beautiful young heifers. All the time he spoke, I imagined I saw a twinkle in Junior's eyes. Just as I thought, he understood every word he heard.

So I put my arm around him and whispered in his ear, "Junior, this is the best thing for each of us and I will come to see you once in a while."

Junior

He understood and, obedient as always, he followed me into the farmer's truck. I tied him up, gave him a couple of hugs and walked off. He turned for a last look at me, never realizing we would never see each other again.

I consoled myself by rationalizing that Junior, after siring many a beautiful offspring, finally would go to the great white apple orchard in the sky or wherever good bulls go when they leave this world. He would go quietly and serenely with the memory of those lovely young heifers and he would go with a smile on his face.

About the Author

Lou Bader's family came to Flagstaff, Arizona in 1914. The population at that time was about 1,500. Most of the stories, as seen through the eyes of a little boy, were written primarily for the benefit of his 15 grandchildren; only because of the efforts of Mr. Joseph Karol have they become public. Mr. Karol is an instructor in English composition at Northern Arizona University, Flagstaff.

Lou has had a diversified career. This is his first attempt at writing. His main interest in his later years has been in bronze sculpting. Lou makes bronze come alive. In his skilled hands, cold metal becomes warm, animated figures in flight, in movement, in evolution. From his hands, bronze acquires personality, substance and feeling. A freeze-frame of life is mirrored by his works.

A gentle, sensitive man, Bader's inner intensities are revealed in his work. From an Indian warrior hooded in wolfskin to a primitive, stylized African deer, Bader's work projects a depth and richness seldom seen in contemporary castings.

Born in Cincinnati, Ohio, and raised in the rugged logging town of Flagstaff, Arizona, Bader gained an early respect for animals and all living creatures. This affinity for other creatures is evident in the highly detailed muscles of a bronze horse, the fur of a bear and the curve of the feather of an eagle in flight. In these representations, Bader reveals his immense perception of detail, movement and form.

His talents include experimentations with other media, much of it occurring naturally in the pristine areas surrounding Flagstaff. Melding bronze with lava, wood bark, or malpais rock, Bader constantly seeks new expressions for his love of textures and designs.

Bader turned his attention from wood sculpting to bronze casting only a few years ago. Essentially self-taught, Bader quickly learned that the limits of his capabilities stretched only as far as his imagination. His three impressive life-sized dolphins created for a hospital in Texas, seem to defy gravity as they skim golden waves.

His most magnificent piece to date is an eagle in flight, literally a gift of love to Flagstaff Medical Center. Bader's strong sense of community spirit and civil loyalty led him to create the eagle for donation to the hospital. Hospital officials and the Board of Trustees were stunned by his generosity.

"The eagle is a symbol of strength, security and America," Bader said.

Lou Bader's career has spanned a cross-section of the arts. A professional singer on radio and stage, a television personality and movie director/producer (*The Magnificent Mullato*) Bader's personal creativity has flourished in a multitude of media. In addition, he has produced and directed at the Pasadena Playhouse, the Burbank Civic Light Opera and the Glendale Light Opera.

A building contractor, realtor, aircraft designer and former county commissioner, Bader's civic and professional interests are also varied. A subdivision near the lovely San Francisco Peaks in Flagstaff was created by the artist and bears his name – Baderville.

Bader's delicate "Ponderosa Madonna" won first prize at the Festival of the Madonnas in Beverly Hills, California. Other firsts were awarded in Eagle Rock, Glendale, Burbank, Los Angeles and Houston. Additional recognition has come from local fairs and exhibits, as well as in magazines and other publications.

Artisan, philosopher, philanthropist, builder and community leader, Lou Bader is truly a modern-day Renaissance man.

His latest art work of bronze is a gift to the city of Flagstaff. A life-sized eagle, fawn and mountain man can be seen on the lawn of the City Hall. Lou is married to Emma Jean Babbitt, granddaughter of David Babbitt, who contributed so much to the successful growth of Flagstaff.

Light Opera period
Burbank Light Opera

Singing and acting
period

Lou the director

Lou, 1988

Lou and daughter, Antoinette
Concert period

"Frontier Adventure"
Flagstaff City Hall

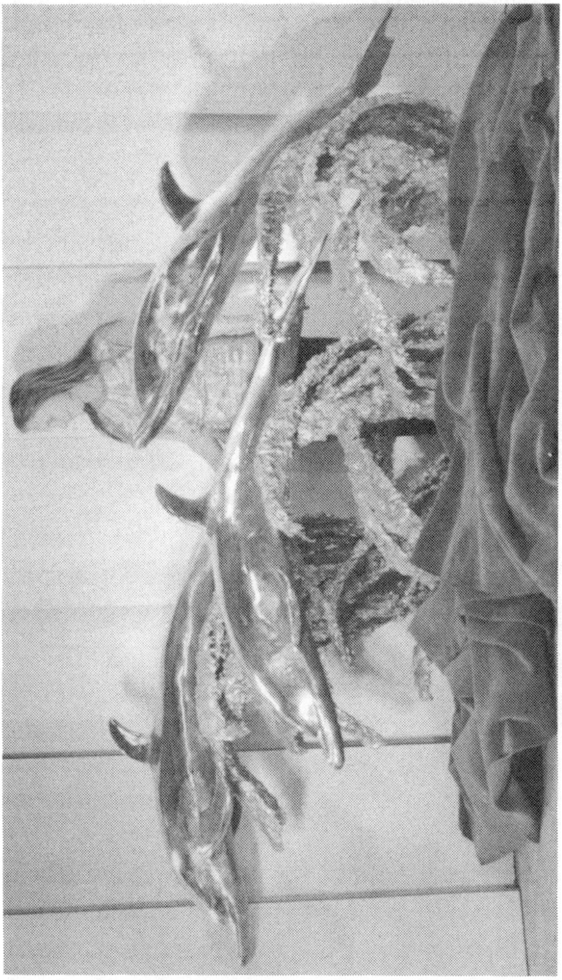

Emma Jean Bader and Golden Dolphins
in the Baderville Studio

Dolphins at San Jacinto Methodist Hospital

Subject dictated by natural form in wood

Ponderosa Madonna
Wood carving by Lou

Fighter plane model designed by Lou while working at Lockheed Aerodynamic Research Laboratory during Korean War